MOLIÈRE

Tartuffe
AND
The Misanthrope

Jean-Baptiste Poquelin de
MOLIÈRE

Tartuffe

AND

The Misanthrope

Translated, with Notes, by Prudence L. Steiner
Introduced by Roger W. Herzel

Hackett Publishing Company, Inc.
Indianapolis/Cambridge

Copyright © 2009 by Hackett Publishing Company, Inc.
All rights reserved

Printed in the United States of America
14 13 12 11 10 09   1 2 3 4 5 6 7

For further information, please address
Hackett Publishing Company, Inc.
P.O. Box 44937
Indianapolis, Indiana 46244-0937

www.hackettpublishing.com

Cover design by Abigail Coyle
Interior design by Elizabeth L. Wilson
Composition by William Hartman
Printed at Malloy, Inc.

Library of Congress Cataloging-in-Publication Data
  Molière, 1622–1673.
    [Tartuffe. English]
    Tartuffe ; and, The misanthrope / Jean-Baptiste Poquelin de Moliére ; translated, with notes, by Prudence L. Steiner ; introduced by Roger W. Herzel.
       p. cm.
    ISBN 978-1-60384-128-3 (cloth) —
    ISBN 978-1-60384-127-6 (pbk.)
    1. Molière, 1622–1673—Translations into English. 2. French drama—Translations into English.   I. Steiner, Prudence L.   II. Molière, 1622–1673. Misanthrope. English.   III. Title.
  PQ1842A478 2009
  842'.4—dc22   2009017349

The paper used in this publication meets the minimum requirements of American National Standard for Information Sciences—Permanence of Paper for Printed Library Materials, ANSI Z39.48–1984.

Contents

General Introduction   vii

Translator's Note: *Tartuffe*   4

    Molière's Preface, March 1669   6

Tartuffe   12

Notes to *Tartuffe*   119
First Appeal to the King   128
Second Appeal to the King   131
Third Appeal to the King   133

Translator's Note: *The Misanthrope*   138

The Misanthrope   141

Notes to *The Misanthrope*   233

General Introduction

Tartuffe and *The Misanthrope* are the two most famous plays by Molière, whom many consider the world's greatest comic playwright, and the two that are most frequently read in literature classes and performed by university and professional theater companies in the United States. The plot of each play is strong, clear, and timeless: in the first, the scoundrel Tartuffe, through a hypocritical display of religious piety, gains so much influence over the wealthy bourgeois Orgon that he very nearly succeeds in ruining Orgon's entire family; but at the end Tartuffe is exposed, the sympathetic characters triumph, and life returns to normal. In the second, Alceste the misanthrope, the man who hates humankind, denounces the falseness and insincerity of the society in which he lives, but nevertheless he is in love with Célimène, who embodies the very faults that he condemns in others; he demands that she prove her love for him by leaving the social world of Paris, but she refuses and their relationship dissolves.

The two plays are almost totally unlike each other. If it were necessary to choose one play as a typical example of Molière's work, and of the rich tradition of European comedy, *Tartuffe* would probably be the choice; *The Misanthrope* stands alone in a category by itself. And yet there are strong links between the plays: both are centrally concerned with the subject of hypocrisy, *The Misanthrope* seems to have been written at least partly in response to the turmoil aroused by *Tartuffe,* and for centuries they have been Molière's two most controversial works. The controversy over each play, but in different ways, arises from the subject. Of all the vices that have been portrayed on stage,

General Introduction

hypocrisy is the most overtly theatrical, since it involves playing a role, pretending to be someone other than one's true self. Indeed the vice takes its name from the ancient Greek word for "acting." The ordinary pleasure that theater audiences take in watching a good actor play a character acquires an extra dimension when the character, in turn, is playing a role within the fictional world of the play. In the real world, of course, the spectacle of hypocrisy inspires contempt rather than pleasure: Tartuffe in real life would be a despicable person, but on stage it is fun to watch him work—partly because his actions are fictional, partly because the playwright can show the contradictions between Tartuffe's real and pretended selves with a clarity that is not often available in real life. The controversy over this play concerns the tone and intention of Molière's comedy: was he, through the religious hypocrite Tartuffe, by implication attacking the religious establishment in general? The archbishop of Paris thought so, and he threatened excommunication for anyone who saw, read, or listened to a reading of the play; and one excitable priest declared that Molière should be burned at the stake (as had been done to a heretic in Paris the previous year). In *The Misanthrope* the controversy is less inflammatory but more basic: Is the person who denounces hypocrisy entirely sincere himself? Is he admirable or ridiculous—or a little of both? Is the play a comedy at all, or should we interpret it as a sort of tragedy?

Any reader of the printed play engages in an act of interpretation, as do the director and the actors who put on a production of it, as well as the audience, who must further interpret the director's interpretation. What follows is not an attempt to impose any particular interpretation upon the reader but to point out some of the major questions and to provide information that may help in enjoying and interpreting the plays.

Molière's Life

Perhaps the most important thing that can be said about Molière is that he was an actor before he was an author. "Molière" was the name he adopted for the stage. He was born as Jean-Baptiste Poquelin in January 1622 in the heart of Paris, near the markets. His father, like both his grandfathers, was a *tapissier*—an upholsterer and interior decorator, who had prospered greatly in his business and secured an appointment at court. It was understood that the son would inherit the father's business and royal appointment, and he was well and expensively educated in preparation for that career.

His boyhood home was near the two professional theaters operating in Paris. The longer-established of these, the troupe of actors performing at the Hôtel de Bourgogne, was noteworthy for a brilliant trio of farce-players. Their leader Gros-Guillaume ("Fat William"), a popular favorite, played rustic and naive characters, dressed in a flat cap, striped trousers, and a loose tunic secured by two belts above and below his impressive belly; his moonface was whitened with flour. He was joined by the long-legged and extremely thin Gaultier-Garguille, who played the old man, wearing a black costume, large spectacles, and a mask with a long, pointed beard; he was said to move like a perfectly controlled marionette. The third member, Turlupin, was well built and handsome; he also wore a mask, and he played sharp, knavish characters. There is a legend, unsubstantiated but perfectly plausible, that Jean-Baptiste's grandfather took him to see this trio perform; any memories he would retain would be early ones, however, because the first of the trio died when Molière was eleven and the last when he was fifteen.

The other company, recently arrived in Paris and playing at the Théâtre du Marais, had the French theater's first genuine star actor and its first great playwright. A few days before Molière's fifteenth birthday these two combined in the opening of Corneille's *The Cid*, officially called a "tragedy" but perhaps better described as a romantic adventure-play about love and honor; the passionate, charismatic Montdory played the title role. The opening of this play was one of the great events in French literary history, as it changed the course of French drama and for the first time attracted a wealthy, educated, and fashionable audience to the theater.

In 1643, when Jean-Baptiste was twenty-one years old, he signed legal documents renouncing his right to inherit his father's business and joined a young acting company that was rashly trying to establish itself in competition with the Théâtre du Marais and Hôtel de Bourgogne. The troupe, calling itself the Illustre Théâtre, "Illustrious Theater," was headed by a remarkable woman named Madeleine Béjart, four years older than Molière (as he soon began to call himself)—a powerful actress, talented writer, shrewd businesswoman, and free spirit who was Molière's lover for a time and remained an actress in his company until her death in 1672, one year to the day before his own. Her brother and sister were among the ten members of the original acting company, and two more family members joined it in later years. After two years of struggling to make a living in Paris, the troupe left for the provinces. Little is known of the next thirteen years; the troupe moved from town to town, normally performing double bills of a five-act main play followed by a one-act farce afterpiece, losing some actors along the way and gaining others. When they returned to Paris in October 1658, with Molière now the head of the troupe, only he and the three Béjarts remained from the original company. An audition before the twenty-year-old king Louis XIV had been arranged by the king's brother; the main play, a tragedy by Corneille, was not well received, but the afterpiece, a farce called *The Doctor in Love*, so amused the king that he granted permission for the troupe to perform in Paris and allowed them to use, on alternate days, the theater occupied by the *commedia dell'arte* company headed by Scaramouche. This arrangement gave Molière the opportunity to observe and learn from the masters of Italian comedy.

At this point, more than halfway through his thirty-year career in the theater, Molière was not in any significant sense a playwright: he had written only two full-length plays and had written, borrowed, or adapted a number of short French and Italian farces, of which only two survive. Nor did he think of himself as a specialist in comedy, though this was clearly what he was best at. Comic skills were useful to an actor because they pleased the audience; but comedy was considered a markedly inferior form of theater, and for an ambitious actor the way to gain prestige was through tragic and heroic roles—or, in the vocabulary of the time, "serious" theater. Molière had been reasonably successful in such roles in the provinces, but in Paris he was ridiculed for his ungainly bearing, his choppy vocal delivery, and above all for his insistence on employing a "natural," conversational style in serious plays, like those of Corneille, that were written in an idealized and declamatory mode.

But these same qualities, when employed in the performance of comedy, won him the entire approval of the Paris audience, who had seen nothing like him before; and he began to write new plays—twenty-nine of them over the next fourteen years— that made use of his own talents in the central comic role and that, just as importantly, exploited the abilities of his supporting cast. Writing style was inseparable from acting style: his scripts, based on sharp observation of contemporary Parisian social behavior rather than the conventional and artificial world of earlier comedy, required his troupe's "natural" delivery. Molière's contemporaries were struck by the apparent lack of artifice in the performances of his actors: "they seem to be born for all the characters they portray."[1]

Molière's first years in Paris were marked by daring experimentation and the continual effort to try new material in each play instead of repeating himself. The only interruption in this string of successes was his one attempt at a "heroic" play, *Dom Garcie de Navarre* (1661), which was a complete and humiliating failure for him as an actor and a playwright; but he bounced back

---

1. Gabriel Guéret, quoted in Roger Herzel, *The Original Casting of Molière's Plays* (Ann Arbor: UMI Research Press, 1981), 57.

quickly from this disaster with two more innovative comedies in the same year, *The School for Husbands*, the first of his "character comedies," and *The Bores*, commissioned as part of a lavish entertainment for the king. This was the first of the "comedy-ballets," a hybrid form in which comic scenes performed by professional actors provided breaks and time for costume changes between dances performed by Louis' courtiers; the scenes Molière provided were caricatures of courtly eccentrics—a hunter, a card-player, a pedant, and so on—of whom Molière played four. The success of this venture led to a series of demands by the king for Molière to provide entertainment for festivals at Versailles and the other royal residences.

In 1662 he produced the play that definitively established him as not just an entertainer but a literary author to be taken seriously: *The School for Wives*, a verse play in five acts, which was the norm for "high" drama. It was a *tour de force* for himself, La Grange, and Catherine de Brie, the troupe's three best actors, and a great success with audiences. But Molière's good fortune over the past few years had earned him some enemies—people in society who viewed his satirical brand of comedy as threatening, and rival actors at the Hôtel de Bourgogne who had grown increasingly resentful of his success and his favor with the king; and when some moralists claimed to find the play indecent and impious, on the basis of some very mild sexual innuendo and a scene that can be interpreted as a parody of the Ten Commandments, his enemies blew this into a storm of controversy, with printed pamphlets and polemical afterpieces, that lasted two years (and, incidentally, increased attendance at both theaters). Earlier in the year Molière, at the age of forty, had married the nineteen-year-old Armande Béjart, who was either the sister or, as most believe, the daughter of Madeleine; she now made her acting debut in the two plays that Molière contributed to the controversy, *The Critique of the School for Wives* and *The Versailles Impromptu*. Montfleury, the leading tragic actor of the Hôtel de Bourgogne, whom Molière satirized in these plays, was so enraged that he accused Molière of having married his own daughter; the king, to whom this complaint was addressed, responded by standing godfather to the couple's first child and by commissioning and dancing in the performance at the Louvre of Molière's second comedy-ballet, *The Forced Marriage*.

The controversy over *The School for Wives* was just beginning to die down when, in May 1664, Louis XIV summoned Molière to provide entertainment for a massive, seven-day festival inaugurating his splendid new château and park in Versailles. The troupe was kept busy, participating in a costumed parade and a ballet and presenting revivals of *The Bores* and *The Forced Marriage* plus two new plays: *The Princess of Elide* and *Tartuffe*. This was not the same *Tartuffe* that we now read, because it was a play in three acts rather than the eventual five; how it differed from the final version is of course a question that has given rise to much lively speculation, since it was the three-act version that was considered offensive enough to be banned. I will return to this question in more detail later; but for the moment, it is fair to say that it probably would not have mattered much what the earliest version was like, since opposition to the play was already forming a full month before it was first performed. The Company of the Holy Sacrament, a secret society with ties to many powerful individuals, including the king's mother, resolved in mid-April to work for the suppression of the play; and though Louis himself found the performance "very amusing," within a few days of the performance he banned the play—temporarily, until it could be completely finished and examined by experts—making it clear that Louis was confident of Molière's good intentions but concerned that some spectators might not be able, as Louis himself was, to distinguish between true and false piety. Religious tensions were high at the moment, the subject matter of the play was potentially explosive, and the king, in dealing with the crisis, acted like both a statesman and a politician. This temporary ban lasted for more than five years.

The opposition may not have caught Molière by surprise, but the ban certainly did. The crisis was both artistic and financial: the troupe needed new plays to produce income, and something had to take the place of *Tartuffe*. Two more great plays on the theme of hypocrisy followed. In *Don Juan* (1665) La Grange played the charming, amoral seducer and Molière the nattering, moralistic valet who attempts in vain to dissuade Don Juan from his life of sin. Denunciations from the pulpit were thunderous, focusing on Molière's performance. Attendance was excellent, but for reasons we can only guess at, the play abruptly vanished from the repertory and was never revived in Molière's lifetime. In *The Misanthrope* (1666) Molière played Alceste, who prides himself on his sincerity and who perceives and denounces hypocrisy everywhere in contemporary fashionable life; he continually threatens to withdraw from society but contradicts his principles by his love for the elusive, coquettish Célimène, who embodies all of society's faults. The play is comic but ends in sadness and frustration.

Always the experimenter, Molière in *The Misanthrope* had gone as far as he could go in exploring the possibilities of comic realism, and this play marks a watershed in his career: after it he wrote only one more "regular" play—that is, a five-act play in verse—and prose, visual spectacle, and fantasy dominated the second half of his career. Most of Molière's later plays defy traditional classification: even *The Doctor in Spite of Himself*, the next play after *The Misanthrope*, is a play-within-a-play, a *commedia dell'arte* plot framed by a native French farce, while *The Tricks of Scapin* is both a throwback to *commedia* and a parody of it. Two of his most enduringly popular plays, *The Would-Be Gentleman* (1670) and *The Imaginary Invalid* (1673), combine the characteristics of the comedy-ballet and character comedy; in each play the ending, instead of restoring the deluded central character to reality (as Orgon is restored in *Tartuffe*), carries him off in a final ballet sequence into the realms of permanent fantasy.

During that ballet in the fourth performance of *The Imaginary Invalid*, Molière, playing the role of the perfectly healthy man who imagines that he is ill, was stricken with a fatal hemorrhage of the lungs; he finished the show and died at home a few hours later. The Church, implacable to the last, refused to allow him to be buried; then, under pressure from the king, permitted burial at night without a service.

After his death, the troupe was held together by La Grange and Molière's widow, Armande. Four actors defected to the Hôtel de Bourgogne, and the remaining ones joined forces with the actors of the Théâtre du Marais. After seven years this combined company merged again, by order of the king, with the Hôtel de Bourgogne; thus the number of theaters in Paris had been reduced from three to one, which soon became known as the Comédie-Française.

Tartuffe in Three Acts and Five

Tartuffe as originally played, and banned, at Versailles was a three-act play. What was it like? Various answers have been proposed, all of them somewhat unsatisfactory and none of them provable. La Grange wrote in his notebook (probably after the fact) that the troupe performed "three acts of *Tartuffe* which were the three first";[2] if we take this at face value it means that Louis saw Acts I, II, and III of the play we now have. Here is a brief summary of the plot by act:

> **Act I.** Orgon, a rich bourgeois of Paris, has become so infatuated with the ostentatious piety of Tartuffe that he has showered him with gifts and brought him to live in his house, to the dismay of most of the rest of the family, who consider Tartuffe a fraud. **Act II.** Orgon announces that he will give his daughter Mariane in marriage to Tartuffe, breaking his promise to her fiancé Valère, whom she deeply loves. **Act III.** Elmire, Orgon's young second wife, intercedes with Tartuffe to try to persuade him to give up the plan of marrying Mariane; he responds by declaring his desire

---

2. *Registre de La Grange 1659–1685*, ed. Bert Edward Young and Grace Philputt Young (Paris: Droz, 1947), 67.

for Elmire and making a crude pass at her. Damis, Orgon's son, has overheard this scene and denounces Tartuffe to his father; but Orgon refuses to believe any ill of Tartuffe, throws Damis out of the house, and instructs Tartuffe to spend as much time as possible with Elmire. **Act IV.** Elmire persuades Orgon to see with his own eyes if Tartuffe is a traitor; Orgon hides under a table while Tartuffe attempts again to seduce Elmire, emerging only when he hears Tartuffe call him a gullible fool. He orders Tartuffe out of the house, but Tartuffe replies that the house belongs to him because Orgon has given him the title, along with a box of other documents. **Act V.** Tartuffe has dispossessed the family of everything they own. An officer arrives to arrest Orgon for treason, on the basis of that box of documents; but instead he arrests Tartuffe, because the king knows of his bad character and will not allow fraud to succeed. The family is rescued, and Mariane will marry Valère.

The first question is whether the troupe presented the play to Louis and his guests as a complete work or a work-in-progress. The latter suggestion seems highly implausible: such an ostentatious social and political occasion would not be a good time to ask the audience to watch something that Molière was "working on." Does this mean that something corresponding very closely to Acts I, II, and III of the play we have was presented as a complete work? Strong arguments have been made in favor of this idea; the play would thus end with Tartuffe victorious and Orgon the (unconscious) victim; Tartuffe's seduction of Elmire and cuckolding of his benefactor would occur after the final curtain and be left to the imagination of the audience, but the point would be clear enough. The play would be, in short, an old-fashioned farce. The difficulties are that there would be no follow-up to the Mariane plot, making Act II irrelevant; and that Tartuffe would be on stage for only one of the three acts.

An alternative proposal suggested by John Cairncross has received a good deal of favorable attention: that the play as first presented consisted of something very close to Acts I, III, and IV of the present version.³ Thus Tartuffe is on stage for two-thirds of the play; he is exposed and defeated at the end of the wonderful table scene; there is no need for the sudden introduction of the previously unmentioned box of documents, or for the king's miraculous intervention; the play has a smaller cast and a simpler plot, since Mariane and Valère do not appear and there would be no discussion of her marrying Tartuffe; but the plot would still end happily with order restored. The entire tone of the play would be much different from the version consisting of Acts I, II, and III.

Needless to say, there is no proof of either theory and this is all pure speculation. It is speculation with a purpose, however, because the plot is the primary guide to a play's meaning, and considering the possibilities for the early version of *Tartuffe* is a way of bringing into focus our interpretation of Molière's intentions in writing the play.

Tartuffe and the Comic Tradition

In the absence of the early version, we can still usefully compare the finished script of *Tartuffe* to the generality of the comic tradition. This was much more familiar and more useful in guiding the expectations of the audience in the seventeenth century than it is today; indeed, from the time of Plautus (and before) until the end of the eighteenth century, comic playwrights tended to use familiar formulas and plot devices over and over again, basing their claims to originality on their success in surprising the audience with fresh variations on a well-established theme.

Probably the oldest comic theme of all is that of one person playing a trick on another, and the audience who witnesses the playing-out of this action is placed in an ambiguous moral position. The trickster is generally someone of a low social

---

3. John Cairncross, *New Light on Molière* (Geneva: Droz, 1956).

position—a servant or slave, an outlaw, or someone with a deservedly bad reputation. The victim is generally someone of the respectable middle class, with power in society. The audience members who laugh at the situation resemble the victim more closely than the trickster, and the victim clearly is morally superior. And yet the audience is always on the side of the trickster, wanting to see him succeed—an opposite response when watching the play to what their response would be to the same events in real life. This suspension of moral disapproval is one of the reasons why strict moralists have always maintained that the theater is a dangerous institution that erodes the audience's sense of right and wrong. The ending of the play makes some difference in the overall moral tone, but not a great deal: if the trickster is defeated and punished at the end, rather than getting away with his dishonesty, it is possible to pretend that the play is not completely cynical but is consistent with conventional morality; the fact remains, however, that while the plot is in progress the audience is laughing *with* the cleverness of the rogue and, even more important, laughing *at* the credulity of the victim. We have examples of both kinds of ending in the two hypothetical structures that have been proposed for the earliest version of *Tartuffe*—Acts I, II, III or Acts I, III, IV—and the difference between them is real. But in either case, of course, the plot in three words is "Tartuffe tricks Orgon," and the fact that he does so by feigning religious piety vastly increases the opportunity for moralists to take offense.

Equally basic to the comic tradition is the ancient plot on which the huge majority of traditional comedies are based, "boy gets girl." In order to fulfill his desires the boy must overcome some obstacle, represented by an older man who has power, and this basic triangle of old man, young man, and young woman is the core of comedy in the European tradition. Other characters in the play are there to serve this conflict; for example, since the young man lacks power, he may decide that he needs to resort to trickery and therefore enlist the aid of that very popular character, the clever servant. The mating plot thus goes hand in hand with the trickery plot. This basic situation is capable of an almost limitless number of variations. For example, the old man may be the boy's father; he has arranged for his son to marry the daughter of his friend—a perfectly wise match from the social and financial point of view; but the son has fallen disastrously in love with a gypsy girl. There is thus a conflict of values between the generations: prudence, respectability, and the kind of wisdom that comes from calculation on the one hand, instinct, impetuosity, and the sex drive on the other. The son in despair calls on the trickster to help him out. Chaos ensues. At the last moment, by chance, it is discovered that the supposed gypsy girl is in fact the long-lost daughter of the father's friend, and all ends happily. The generations are reconciled and the conflict of values disappears, because the instinct of the son had led him to fall in love with the very girl that the prudence of the father had chosen. This is the plot of Molière's *The Tricks of Scapin*, stolen from *Phormio*, a play written eighteen centuries earlier by the Roman playwright Terence. Like most traditional comedies, Molière's and Terence's plays end with a wedding, which is the symbol of reconciliation between sex and respectability in the theater just as it is in real life.

Another possibility is that the young man and the old man can be in direct competition for the possession of the young woman. This is the situation in Molière's early plays *The School for Husbands* and *The School for Wives*, in which the old man is the guardian of the girl and intends to compel her to marry him. This clear abuse of power is thwarted by the young couple, with the girl herself taking on the function of the trickster, and the plays end in marriage; reconciliation between the generations, however, is not possible in this situation, as the happy ending requires the clear defeat of the old authority figure.

But what if the wedding has already taken place before the beginning of the comedy and the old man is the husband, the young woman his discontented wife, and the young man her would-be lover? This is the situation in William Wycherley's famous Restoration comedy *The Country Wife* (1675), adapted from both of Molière's *School* plays. Clearly the only way for the young people to satisfy their desires is to engage in adulterous sex, which they do with considerable gusto. Watching and enjoying this play requires the audience to suspend, at least temporarily, conventional reverence for the sanctity of marriage; and thus the play was considered overtly immoral from the eighteenth century until well into the twentieth. More recent interpretations point out that marriage itself, as practiced among the upper classes in Restoration England, was a cynical and mercenary business with little concern for the happiness of the wife and that pious declarations about its sanctity were themselves a hypocrisy that Wycherley was satirizing. However that may be, the situation in which the young wife and her lover (sometimes the village priest) attempt to cuckold the elderly husband has been frequently used in comedy and farce throughout the centuries; sometimes the young couple succeeds and sometimes not, depending on how much raciness the audience will tolerate, but the plot still depends upon the assumption that marriage is the problem rather than the solution. Molière used the cuckolding plot in two of his shorter plays, and it would have been dominant in either of the hypothetical versions of the first three-act *Tartuffe*.

But beginning with the final version of *Tartuffe* and continuing through many of his greatest plays — *The Miser, The Would-Be Gentleman, The Learned Ladies,* and *The Imaginary Invalid* — the version of the comic plot that Molière made distinctively his own leaves no moral ambiguity. These "comedies of character" are set in prosperous bourgeois families; the young man and young woman are in love with each other from the beginning of the play, they want to marry and may have already obtained parental consent, and their marriage is an unmistakably good thing from every conventional point of view; the eventual announcement of their marriage at the end of the comedy provides a satisfying sense of closure and return to normalcy. The function of the old man, who, as always in comedy, serves as obstacle to the young people's happiness, is personified in this set of plays by the girl's father (with the very interesting exception of *The Learned Ladies*, in which it is the mother), who has become warped by a particular obsession and who wants the daughter to marry a different person who will serve that obsession: piety, thrift, social climbing, intellectual life, or physical health. All of these obsessions (except social climbing) are good things in themselves, but they have become distorted by selfishness, and the choice of husband is based on a desire for the parent's happiness, not the daughter's. The miser wants his daughter to marry someone who will take her without a dowry; the social climber wants her to marry a nobleman; the learned mother, a poet, for the intellectual prestige it will bring the family; the hypochondriac, a medical student (surely the funniest and most incompetent medical student who has ever appeared on the stage), so that the father will always have a doctor on call. The motives of these other parents are perfectly clear. Thus we should ask: why does Orgon want his daughter to marry Tartuffe?

The focus of comic and psychological interest in all of these plays is on the obsessed parent, played in every case (except, again, *The Learned Ladies*) by Molière himself. This is particularly the case in *Tartuffe*. Although Tartuffe is the title character and a very showy role, the real interest of the play is not how Tartuffe tricks Orgon but how and why Orgon allows himself to be tricked—indeed, collaborates so enthusiastically in his own deception. Tartuffe is not a master deceiver: only Orgon and his mother, Madame Pernelle, fall for his act, and all the other characters in the play see through him without difficulty. Yet Orgon does not appear to be a stupid man: he is wealthy, apparently because of his own efforts, and it seems that he had played an important and respected role in bourgeois society—until recently, when he met Tartuffe. Why such a man should blind himself so willfully is one of the most intriguing psychological questions that Molière raises in any of his plays.

The Characters and Actors of *Tartuffe*

All of Molière's "comedies of character" take place within a bourgeois family, but the family in *Tartuffe* is the most extensive, comprising eight members and three generations: the father, Orgon; his children by a deceased wife, Mariane and Damis; his future son-in-law, Valère; his mother, Madame Pernelle; his young second wife, Elmire; Elmire's brother, Cléante; and Mariane's companion, Dorine.

    The character of Orgon, like all the characters in any play by Molière, is inseparable from the actor for whom he wrote the role. In this case that actor was himself. His contemporaries knew him, after he gave up his heroic ambitions, as the leading farce-player in France, and he always played the leading comic character, a list that includes heavy fathers, clever or befuddled valets, hapless husbands, rustics, and silly young noblemen. The constant is what contemporaries called the "naturalness" of his acting style. This term implied a contrast with his predecessors based on an entirely different approach to comic acting. Earlier comedians, like the famous farce-players Molière may have seen in his boyhood, based their success on always presenting the same character name, costume, and bag of tricks, so that the audience always knew what to expect. Molière defied expectation and individualized the name and costume of each character he played. His comic success was not achieved in a vacuum but in his interplay with the other actors in his troupe and their varying styles. His performance on stage was always contrasted with one or several characters who appear relatively normal and well adjusted—in this play, Valère, Elmire, and especially Cléante; on the other hand, he always also included one or two characters in smaller roles whose acting styles were markedly grotesque in some way—Madame Pernelle and Tartuffe. Molière thus occupied the middle place in the spectrum, appearing comic in contrast to the one group, effortless and "natural" in contrast to the other. This was an important strategy, since he was always on stage for more time than any other actor.

General Introduction

Tartuffe is naturally the character who attracts the most attention in any modern production. How will he be played? The range of possible interpretations is very wide, and they can all be justified because the essence of the role is that his external appearance, whatever it may be, is misleading: he is a hypocrite through and through. Thus he can be and often is played as a straight villain, somber, threatening, and dangerous; he could equally well be charming and ingratiating. Whatever choice is made, it has consequences for the dynamics of the play. To reduce the question to its simplest terms: Is he attractive or repulsive? In the great scene in Act IV, he attempts to seduce and virtually to rape Elmire while Orgon, hidden under the table, listens and does nothing as the scene goes on and on; what is Orgon thinking, and how does the audience respond? Is the prospect of sex between Tartuffe and Elmire unthinkable and her predicament horrifying, or does it remind the audience of the old farce triangle between the pretty wife, her handsome lover, and her decrepit husband? In the original production the role was written for Du Croisy, who began his career playing young lovers and seems to have been handsome in a fleshy way; Dorine (who, of course, does not like him) describes him as fat, ruddy-complexioned, rosy-lipped, and self-indulgent in his appetites, eating and drinking hugely, belching, snoring—a comic contrast to his self-proclaimed image as an ascetic. Tartuffe was by far the biggest role Du Croisy ever played: he had a ponderous, overemphatic style of speaking, stressing every syllable, that was highly comic in small doses, and he was very useful as a bit-part player, claiming the center of attention during his brief times on stage in dialect roles or as poets and pedants.

Madame Pernelle, Orgon's mother, is the only other character in the play who is deceived by Tartuffe. She is an ill-tempered, impetuous, sharp-tongued, malicious old woman, and like all elderly female characters in seventeenth-century France, she was played by a man. This actor, Louis Béjart, was Madeleine's younger brother, who only played small roles in Molière's plays. A quarrelsome person, he had received a wound in a sword fight that left him with a pronounced limp, and he was something of a favorite with audiences as a result; actors in the provinces playing roles he had originated were said to imitate his limp. It is no coincidence that the first thing we see in the play is this character in violent motion, limping onto the stage so quickly that Elmire cannot keep up: it is a grotesque image, made more so by the fact that it is a travesty role. The year after *Tartuffe* opened, Béjart retired from the theater at the age of forty-five to pursue a new career in the army.

Cléante, Elmire's brother, has no blood relation to Orgon's children but takes a kindly interest in them as an adoptive uncle. His somewhat detached perspective makes him the most reasonable character in the play, which is a rather thankless task for an actor but an important one in maintaining the play's balance. Molière was fortunate in having for this role a versatile actor with a strong stage presence, La Thorillière, who played kings, peasants, or energetic comic roles as needed, in addition to roles such as Cléante that called for eloquence and social grace.

The young lovers, Mariane and Valère, have a rather limited role in this play, appearing only in Acts II and V. As we have seen, it is possible that they were not part of the original conception of the play when it was first presented at Versailles, and when Molière revised it to make it more acceptable to his moralist critics, the insertion of the positive message of their love story, along with the effusive tribute to the king at the very end, may have been part of his strategy. The roles were played by two of Molière's most valuable actors, Catherine de Brie and La Grange, who began their careers playing young-lover roles similar to these and grew into more complex and interesting assignments. La Grange, with his poised and gracious demeanor, was Molière's favorite foil to set off his own acting style; over the course of their careers, these two played more scenes together, by a wide margin, than any other pair of actors.

Damis, Orgon's hotheaded son, bears a strong family resemblance to his father and grandmother. These three are the only characters in the play with a tendency to physical violence: Damis wants to fight Tartuffe, Madame Pernelle slaps her servant, and Orgon tries, but comically fails, to slap Dorine. André Hubert, who created the role, often played nervous, unstable characters who echoed the mannerisms of Molière's characters. After Louis Béjart retired in 1670, Hubert took over the role of Madame Pernelle and went on to achieve fame as a female impersonator, much more subtle and realistic than Béjart.

Elmire, Orgon's young wife, was played by Molière's own young wife, Armande. She had a simple directness to her acting style that, paradoxically, served her well in her most famous role, the elusive, coquettish Célimène in *The Misanthrope*. This style is also evident in the role of Elmire, a grounded, self-possessed young woman who keeps her head even in very trying situations and who, unlike the stepmother of fairy tales, is on good terms with Mariane and Damis and seems to be about the same age.

The fact that the mother of Orgon's children is dead and that he has remarried was so common in the seventeenth century that it needed no explanation: childbirth was dangerous for both mother and baby. There is an additional reason why mothers of grown children appear very rarely as characters in comedy: actresses were unwilling to date themselves as members of the older generation, and such roles had to be played by men—as Hubert did with great success in *The Would-Be Gentleman* and *The Learned Ladies*. Both the social and the theatrical realities need to be kept in mind when considering Dorine, a character difficult to categorize in modern terms. Molière identifies her as Mariane's "suivante," perhaps best translated as "paid companion." She is an employee of the household, but her status is higher than that of a "servant." How old was Mariane when her mother died? We do not know, but Dorine is the closest thing to a mother that Mariane has. She belongs to a large and varied category of women in early modern life and literature who, despite their respectable social origins, lack the financial means to marry within their own class and are thus reduced to a twilight existence as companion, spinster cousin or aunt, duenna, or governess to the daughters of the more financially fortunate. The "suivante" role is common in early French comedy because, unlike the mother, it implies no particular age and can also be played by actresses who are not well suited to young-lover roles. This was the situation of Madeleine Béjart, Molière's first mentor in the theater, his constant companion, and perhaps the mother of his wife. She was an excellent, authoritative actress, best suited for tragic roles but with limited options in comedy; she played a number of "suivantes" and, in several farces, formed a sort of Punch and Judy team with Molière as his quarrelsome wife; there are echoes of this in Act II.

The Misanthrope: Comedy or Tragedy?

As we saw in discussing *Tartuffe,* the traditional comic plot is a powerful tool for guiding the audience's response to a play. *The Misanthrope* does not employ this plot: the play ends not in fulfillment but in frustration. And while some of the minor characters are recognizable comic types—the vain poet, the silly courtier, the prude—the major characters are not. Alceste is antisocial, and comedy is traditionally unsympathetic to antisocial characters. But he is also an idealist; should we therefore admire him and feel his pain when he is disappointed in love?

An eyewitness account of the first production, with Molière in the role of Alceste, suggests that while the overall effect of the performance was comic, the original audience was somewhat perplexed: it was "all the more admirable because the hero is the comic character without being too ridiculous and because he makes well-bred people laugh without telling low, stale jokes such as we are accustomed to seeing in comedies. . . . Despite [Alceste's] madness, if one may call it that, he has the character of a gentleman. . . . Though he seems somewhat ridiculous, he says things that are very just. It is true that he seems to demand too much."⁴ Clearly this witness found it necessary to reconcile conflicting impressions; nevertheless, Alceste was performed by Molière as a comic character.

But that interpretation died with him; in France over the next three centuries, the tradition became well established of performing Alceste in accordance with an uncritical acceptance of his own self-evaluation: as the noble crusader against a corrupt society. This interpretation required the actor to suppress or downplay the many instances of self-contradiction in Alceste's behavior, some of which call his sincerity into question; and sincerity, of course, is Alceste's one claim to distinction.

Since Alceste's war with society is inextricably linked to his relationship with Célimène, this interpretation also required all sympathy to shift away from her and to Alceste: she became cold, cruel, and manipulative, and he became her victim. This interpretation, however misogynistic it may be, can be theatrically effective; but it cuts off exploration of much of the richness and ambiguity of Molière's text.

The Characters and Actors of *The Misanthrope*⁵

It is very important to *Tartuffe* that most of the characters are members of a large extended family. It is equally important to *The Misanthrope*—and very uncharacteristic of Molière—that family relationships (except for the fact that Célimène and Éliante are cousins) are nonexistent. These characters do not have to deal with each other the way family members do; the only thing that

---

4. Jean Donneau de Visé, "Lettre écrite sur la comédie du 'Misanthrope,'" in Molière, *Œuvres complètes*, ed. Georges Couton (Paris: Pléiade, 1972), II: 139.
5. For more detailed discussion of this subject see Roger W. Herzel, "'Much Depends on the Acting': The Original Cast of *Le Misanthrope*," *PMLA* 95 (1980): 348–66.

ties them together is their desire to be in each other's company, and when that desire dissipates they go their separate ways.

What is it that ties Alceste and Célimène together? Are they suited to each other? Does she love him? That question is raised repeatedly within the play and never conclusively answered. Does he love her? The tendency is to automatically assume that he does, but the question is worth asking nevertheless. There is room for much speculation about these questions; in any given production, the answers will be suggested by the way the roles are cast and the decisions the actors make.

The play gives us two important pieces of information about Célimène: she is twenty years old and she is a widow. Her situation would not have been particularly rare in real life: very young women were routinely married off to older men, and death could come suddenly. But in the context of early modern comedy, which envisions women as daughters to be wooed or wives to be seduced, her situation is almost unique. Her husband is dead and apparently unmourned; there is no mention of her father; like Olivia in Shakespeare's *Twelfth Night,* Célimène is mistress of her household and herself. She is young, rich, and free; Alceste, Oronte, Acaste, and Clitandre want to marry her, and all four believe that it is her moral obligation to declare her preference among them. But that obligation exists in the minds of the men; from her own point of view, what incentive is there to marry anyone just now? She has already had a marriage, and it is a safe bet that it was arranged and loveless. If she marries again she will lose her freedom; even if she publicly declares that one of the four is her favorite, she will lose her power, which depends on her ability to keep all four interested and guessing. Her behavior may be selfish; but the fact that she is not a saint does not make her an ogress, as many productions have implied.

What does she think of Alceste? The question has been dangled before the audience throughout the play, without an answer. At the very end of the play he renounces her and she leaves the stage. Surely this is the moment, in her exit speech, when she will at last reveal her feelings. But she has no exit speech—though stage protocol of the time demands one, and every other character in the scene has had one. She just leaves, in an uncomfortable silence in which every eye in the audience is fixed on her. Some clue as to her state of mind will necessarily be conveyed by her carriage, her posture, her body language, her face, her fan; the range of possibilities is very wide, but the text provides no guidance and the interpretation is in the hands of the director and the actress.

This role—one of the most prized in the French repertoire—was written for Molière's wife, Armande (who herself became a widow at the age of thirty). In all of the roles that he wrote for her she is charming, lively, direct, and straightforward; sometimes sharp-tongued, but never devious or evasive—except perhaps under the extreme duress of Elmire's encounters with Tartuffe. That is the image that Armande projected while she was on stage. But that is not the only basis for our perception of Célimène. At the beginning of the play Philinte describes her as an untrustworthy coquette—he and Alceste agree on this point, though they agree on nothing else—and at the end her double-dealing is exposed through her letters. Thus the audience's overall perception of the character is made up of two sharply contrasting components.

Alceste is her mirror image. His principles are clearly and emphatically stated; but his words and actions undercut them at every turn—in his encounter with Oronte, his threatening to leave the stage and then staying, his abject begging of Célimène for reassurances that he has already said he would not believe. Both characters embody contradictions: one appears to be sincere but is not, the other preaches sincerity but does not perform it. Whether it is fair to attach the label of hypocrisy to one or the other or both is a matter of interpretation. But in any case they are a perfectly matched couple, each designed to bring out the worst in the other.

Alceste was, of course, played by Molière himself; I have already quoted from Donneau de Visé's description of his performance. Early in his career he had aspirations to success as an actor in noble and heroic roles; but the Parisian audience found his appearance, vocal delivery, and acting style inadequate to those roles, and he became a specialist in comedy. It is tempting to see the role of Alceste as Molière's attempt to reconcile his new success with his old ambitions, but it is not plausible that he strayed very far from his proven comic skills; and we should keep these skills in mind as we imagine Alceste trying, with increasing frustration, to woo the poised and self-confident Célimène by railing against her unworthiness.

Molière's comic performance in general depended on the interplay he had developed over the years with the other members of his company; and the most important of these was La Grange. His role of Philinte in this play is a much better indicator of his value than the much smaller role of Valère in *Tartuffe*. After Molière himself, he was the troupe's leading actor. In the savage theatrical world of seventeenth-century Paris, no one had a word to say against him; his contemporaries were unanimous in their praise of his vitality and his unstudied grace — qualities that they associated with both the actor and the man. The scenes between Philinte and Alceste show the contrast between two images: La Grange, who, in voice, carriage, and demeanor, offered the audience an idealized vision of its own social behavior, and Molière, whose behavior, both vocal and gestural, was marked by exaggerated strokes that would strike a jarring and incongruous note in polite society and a comic note on the stage.

The initial conversation between these two is interrupted by the entrance of Du Croisy in the role of Oronte, best known to us as the original Tartuffe. In an earlier play, *The Versailles Impromptu*, set in a rehearsal, Molière had given him these instructions:

> You, you play the poet, and you must fill yourself with this character, indicate that pedantic manner which affects even your dealings with high society, that sententious tone of

voice, and that exactitude in pronunciation which stresses every syllable and doesn't omit a single letter of the most painstaking orthography. (Scene 1, my translation)

The application to the role of Oronte is clear enough, and the passage also makes the point again that Molière always took care to provide foils so that his own acting could occupy a middle ground—"the comic character," in contrast to the more normal La Grange, "without being too ridiculous," in contrast to the more exaggerated Du Croisy.

Célimène's other two suitors provide a contrast of their own, strongly resembling the contrast between La Grange and Molière: La Thorillière (Cléante in *Tartuffe*) poised and graceful as Clitandre, Hubert (Damis in *Tartuffe*) excitable and shrill as Acaste. Hubert had a brilliant career ahead of him as a female impersonator; he was also a wickedly good mimic, a skill that probably added greatly to the scene near the end of the play in which he reads aloud Célimène's incriminating letters.

Marquise Du Parc, who played Éliante, was reputedly the most beautiful woman on the Paris stage and a dignified, though perhaps rather wooden, performer in declamatory tragedy. She had little talent for the give-and-take of Molière's brand of comedy, and *The Misanthrope* was her last play with his company. Shortly afterward she was lured away to the rival company at the Hôtel de Bourgogne by the playwright Racine, who became her lover and wrote for her the title role in the great tragedy *Andromaque*. She was gone from the troupe by the time *Tartuffe* finally opened, but it does not seem likely that she would have had a role in that play in any case.

Perhaps the most psychologically interesting character in the play, after Alceste, is the aging prude Arsinoé, played by Catherine de Brie, the youthful and attractive creator of Mariane in *Tartuffe*. Molière seems always to have entrusted her with the most subtle and complex female role in every play, and the entire body of her work makes her the most valuable of his actresses.

General Introduction

Alceste and Célimène are fascinating and ambiguous characters, and there is no end to the discussion of the mysteries of their relationship. But the supporting characters are vividly and sharply defined, and together they make up a little social world from which both Célimène and Alceste are inseparable.

Setting

The entire action of each play takes place in one room in a house in Paris. This convention is so commonplace in the modern theater that we do not give it a second thought; but it was Molière who invented it. The plays of the Greeks and Romans were performed in open-air theaters, and it was always assumed that the fictional location of the action was likewise outdoors: the space in front of the palace, or the street in front of two or three houses. Any action in tragedy or comedy took place in public. This assumption persisted up to the time of Molière; certain scenes of a play might be set in a room, but never until *The Misanthrope* (1666) and *Tartuffe* (1669) had the setting for a full-length play in a commercial theater portrayed a private, domestic interior space. The novelty of this setting reinforced its importance as a visual symbol of the issues at stake in each play. In *Tartuffe* the stage does not represent a public space; it represents what belongs to Orgon and is the concrete embodiment of his status as a bourgeois—someone who owns property in the city. When Tartuffe threatens to turn Orgon and his family out of the house, he is taking away their entire existence. Likewise, the house symbolizes Tartuffe's status as an intruder: it is the space of the family, and he is not a member of the family. In *The Misanthrope* the stage represents the private space that Célimène controls; anyone who enters does so by her permission. Thus the goal of Alceste as well as each of her other suitors is to be alone with her there, and the rivalry between them takes the form of a territorial struggle.

The frontispieces to the first editions of the two plays give a clear picture of the setting (see pages 3 and 137); although they are drawn by different artists with unequal levels of skill, it is clear that while the backdrops were different for each play, the same wings were used at the side of the stage in each case—a typical example of economizing on the cost of scenery.[6]

Language and Style

Molière wrote some of his plays in verse and some in prose. Prose was the language of farce and "low" comedy, while verse was obligatory for the "high" forms of tragedy and heroic drama, which portrayed idealized and noble characters speaking a heightened language that did not attempt to reproduce the way ordinary people speak in everyday life. The verse form used was the Alexandrine: rhyming couplets of twelve-syllable lines, each line with a break after the sixth syllable. The form was a great deal more flexible than this description makes it sound.

More refined comedy with claims to literary merit also used the Alexandrine, with the same technical characteristics but a closer approach to ordinary conversational speech. This was the form Molière used, brilliantly, in *Tartuffe*, and there are serious difficulties in attempting to translate its effects. The long tradition in French drama of rhymed verse makes it familiar and therefore inconspicuous; in English it is a novelty and a distraction. The rhythms of English speech do not lend themselves as well to a regular stress pattern; unless the actor is very careful, a verse translation can sound bouncy in a way that the French does not. Furthermore, the sounds of the language make rhyme more difficult to achieve in English than in French, and rhymes thus sound more self-consciously clever; and even though many of the characters in *The Misanthrope* spend a good deal of energy trying to be clever, the sense of lightness that rhymed couplets often convey risks overshadowing the genuine bite in

---

6. Roger W. Herzel, "The Decor of Molière's Stage: The Testimony of Brissart and Chauveau," *PMLA* 93 (1978): 925–54.

the characters' conversation. Something is always lost in translation; in translating *Tartuffe* into English prose the danger of loss is perhaps greatest in the long speeches, where the verse patterns help shape the rhetorical builds. But that loss is more than made up for if prose gives a more direct sense of what the characters are feeling and how they are coping with their bizarre situation.

Cleverness is not the goal. A reader familiar with the English comic tradition will find that Molière is funny in a different way. English comedies tend to draw their effects from lines that are funny in themselves, independent of the context. In all of Molière's work there is one such line. His is a different approach to comedy: when a line in his plays draws a laugh from the audience, it is not because the line is witty but because of what it reveals about character and situation, which are the foundations of his enduring popularity in all of the many languages into which his plays have been translated.

Roger W. Herzel

Tartuffe

LE TARTVFFE

Translator's Note: *Tartuffe*

One of the problems in translating Alexandrine couplets is that the meter and rhyme may require the poet to change natural word order, to use extra words, to choose synonyms that will fit both the meaning and the formal constraints. The translator who tries to keep as close as possible to the original runs the risk of producing a text that sounds neither like the original nor like the language of the translation. Sentences may have to be longer or shorter than the original, and the order of words in the sentences may be quite different. Words that are appropriate in the new language may not be the exact equivalents of those in the original language. Idioms in both languages change in meaning and in connotation, especially over the course of three hundred or more years; equivalents are often not literal translations. I have done my best to keep close to Molière's text, but this is not a literal translation.

A second issue is the cultural difference between the reign of Louis XIV, the setting of this play, and the world of the twenty-first century. References to court, to the classics, and to the physical appearance of the characters make this clear, and the details are indicators of character rather than simply stage settings. The formality with which the seventeenth-century French talked to one another (even outside the constraints of drama) is quite foreign to modern ears. Giving a flavor of that formality seemed important, but reproducing it as exactly as possible emphasizes the differences between the two cultures and conceals the universality of the plot, the characters, the issues, the moral reactions, the irony, the humor. I have chosen as neutral a style as possible, trying to avoid turns of phrase, idioms, and

Translator's Note: *Tartuffe*

colloquialisms that would stamp the translation with the flavor of this particular time and place. I have, however, tried to give each character the appropriate voice, from the pomposity of Tartuffe to the nagging tone of Mme. Pernelle.

In preparing this translation I have tried to keep in mind the sound and rhythm of speech as it might be heard on a modern stage. To Molière's contemporaries, who were accustomed to hearing Alexandrine verse, the speech of his characters may have sounded quite unremarkable. I have assumed that Molière's drama, wit, and irony can and must be transmitted, even if the form is prose rather than poetry, colloquial rather than formal.

The faults are mine. Great thanks are due to Walter Kaiser, whose meticulous and generous help at the beginning of this project were of enormous importance and value, and to the *Cercle des Lectrices de Cambridge*, whose comments in the last stages were equally important. I dedicate this translation to my sister, Susan E. Linder, in whose company I first met Molière in Molière's own city.

Molière's Preface
March 1669

This is a comedy about which there has been a lot of talk, which was persecuted for a long time, and those whom it displays made it very clear that they were more powerful in France than those whom I had presented earlier. The marquis, the pretentious folk, the cuckolds, and the doctors, peacefully allowed themselves to be presented on stage; and pretended to have fun—as everyone did—with the portraits that were painted of themselves. But hypocrites do not understand a joke; they were instantly enraged and were appalled that I had the effrontery to present their grimaces and to try to describe a way of life that so many people engage in. Mine was a crime that they could not forgive, and they attacked my comedy with dreadful rage. They did not bother to attack the places that attacked them; they were too clever for that and knew all too well how to prevent themselves from revealing their souls. In their praiseworthy fashion, they concealed their own interests in the name of God; and in their mouths *Tartuffe* became a play that attacks piety. It is, from one end to the other, full of abominations, and there is nothing in it that does not deserve to be burned. Every syllable is blasphemy; even the gestures are sinful; the least glance, the least shake of a head, the smallest step to left or to right hides secrets that they are able to explain in ways that harm me.

Never mind that I submitted it to the judgment of my friends, to the criticism of everyone; despite all the corrections I made, and the opinion of the king and the queen, who saw the play, the approval of great princes and ministers of state who honored the play by their presence, the testimony of right-thinking people who found it useful—all that was of no use. They refused to let go, and even now they continue to provoke the foolish zealots who piously curse me and charitably condemn me.

I would worry very little about what they say were it not for the tricks by which they have made those whom I respect become my enemies, and enticed into their party some truly honorable men on whose goodwill they depend, men who—because of their love of Heaven—are easily made to believe what they are told. This is what required me to defend myself. I want to justify my comedy to the truly pious; and I beseech them, with all my heart, not to condemn things before seeing them, to abandon their preconceptions, not to fall prey to the passions of those whose grimaces are unworthy of them.

If one takes the trouble to examine my comedy in good faith, one will surely see that my intentions were completely innocent, that the play never mocks the things we ought to revere, that I treated my subject with all the precautions that the sensitivity of the subject demanded, and that I used all my art and all the skills I possessed to distinguish clearly between the hypocrite and the truly pious man. I used two acts to prepare for the entrance of my scoundrel. Nothing he did could deceive the listener; he is recognized immediately by the way I presented him; and from beginning to end he says nothing, does nothing, that does not reveal to the spectators the character of a wicked man who can but make the honorable man shine all the more brightly.

I know very well that in rebuttal these gentlemen try to suggest that the theater is not the place to present these matters; but I would ask, with their permission, what is the basis of this worthy assumption? It is a maxim that they can at best assert and that they cannot possibly prove. Indeed, it would not be difficult to show them that comedy, in the ancient world, had its roots in religion and was a part of their sacred mysteries; that our neighbors the Spaniards never celebrate feast days without including a comedy; and that, among ourselves, comedy owes its birth to the efforts of a confraternity to which the House of Burgundy belongs; that the stage was a place set up to present the most important mysteries of our faith; that to this day we see comedies printed in gothic letters under the name of a learned doctor of the Sorbonne; and that, without looking further afield, we have seen in these days the sacred plays of M. Corneille, which have excited the admiration of all of France.

If the task of comedy is to correct the vices of mankind, I do not understand why some of those vices should be exempt. In the State, the vice of hypocrisy is far more dangerous than all the others; and we have seen that the theater is a strong force for its correction. The most beautiful phrases of a serious sermon are frequently less powerful than satire, and nothing alerts men more effectively than the display of their vices. Displaying vice to the mockery of men deals it a great blow. Men put up with admonition but are loath to be mocked. One might be willing to be wicked; one cannot bear to appear foolish.

People attack me for putting pious language in the mouth of an impostor. Well! How could I fail to do this if I wanted to present accurately the character of a hypocrite? It was enough, it seemed to me, to reveal the criminal motives that made him say these things and to have omitted those holy words that it would have been horrible to hear him misuse. But, say they, at the beginning of the fourth act he uses a pernicious and casuistic argument. Yet has not everyone heard such casuistry being used? Does my comedy present anything new? Who could believe that such widely detested behavior would influence anyone; that I make it more dangerous by presenting it on the stage, that it would receive some validity because it is presented by a scoundrel? That does not seem possible, and the comedy of *Tartuffe* should be approved or all comedies banned.

This is the argument that rages so furiously nowadays; never has there been so much agitation against the theater. I do not deny that some Fathers of the Church have condemned comedy, but one cannot also deny that some have discussed it more leniently. Thus the authority that is supposed to support the censure is destroyed by this division of opinion; and the only conclusion one can reach, given this division and also the support of enlightened men, is that they viewed comedy differently; that some discussed it in its purest form while others looked at its corrupted form, confusing it with all those lewd spectacles that are rightly considered indecent.

And in fact, since one must discuss things and not words, and since most disagreements are caused by failing to understand and by using the same word to encompass two different ideas, all that is necessary is to remove the veil of ambiguity and see what comedy is in itself, to see whether it should be condemned. Then, since it is only a clever poem that pleasantly rebukes the defects of mankind, it will be seen that we cannot justly condemn it; and if we are willing to listen to the testimony of the ancients on this subject, we would learn that its most famous philosophers, who claimed so austere a form of wisdom and who ceaselessly attacked the vices of their era, themselves praised comedy. We would learn that Aristotle gave many an evening to the theater and took the trouble to state the principles governing the art of comedy. Antiquity would teach us that its greatest and most revered figures took pride in writing comedies, that others did not scorn to perform those that they had written, that Greece demonstrated its esteem for this art by awarding it prizes and by building the superb theaters in which it was performed, and finally, that in Rome this same art received extraordinary honor—I am not referring to Rome in its debauched state, governed by licentious rulers, but to the disciplined Rome of the times of the consuls, the days of its most strenuous virtue.

I admit that there were times when comedy became corrupt. And what is there in the world that is not constantly being corrupted? There is nothing so innocent that men cannot turn toward vice; no art so beneficial that cannot be distorted; nothing so intrinsically good that it cannot be used for ill. Medicine is a useful art, and everyone honors it as one of the best that we have; and yet there have been times when it was odious and often used to poison. Philosophy[1] is a gift of Heaven, given to us to raise our thoughts to the knowledge of a God through the contemplation of the wonders of nature, and yet we know that it has often been diverted from its proper work and used to support heresy. Even the holiest matters cannot be protected from human corruption, and we see, every day, scoundrels who take advantage of piety and use it wickedly to support the most criminal actions. But this should not prevent us from making important distinctions. We should not confuse the value of things that have been corrupted with the malice of those who corrupt it. Everyone distinguishes between the misuse of an art and the art itself; and since we do not forbid the practice of medicine because it was banned in Rome, nor philosophy because it was condemned in Athens, neither should we forbid comedy because it was censured in times past. This censure was justified for reasons that are no longer relevant. Such censure was constrained by what it was able to see; we must see it in its own terms, understand it as it was then, or ask it to account for innocence as well as corruption. The comedy that this censure attacked has nothing to do with the comedy that we wish to defend. We must take care not to confuse the one with the other. They are two completely different entities with completely different natures. They are similar only in name; it would be a horrifying injustice to condemn Olympia, a virtuous woman, because there was an Olympia who was debauched. Such acts would, without doubt, cause great disorder in the world. In the end, no one would escape condemnation; and since we do not insist on this rigor when we see so many things misused these days, we should be equally generous to comedy and approve those performances designed to demonstrate and teach virtue and honor.

I know that there are some whose sensitivity cannot bear any levity, who say that the most decent comedies are the most dangerous, that the emotions they present are most seductive

---

1. Molière uses "philosophy" both in its present sense and as a synonym for natural sciences, which was common in his day.

because they are virtuous, and that souls are moved by such performances. I do not understand why it is so great a crime to feel moved by honorable passions; and those who want us to be unmoved demand of us an exceptionally high level of virtue. I doubt that such perfection is within the power of human nature, and I do not know whether it is not better to try to correct and to soften the passions of men than it is to eliminate those passions completely. I acknowledge that there are better places to go than to the theater; and if one wants to condemn all activity that does not directly address God and our salvation, it is certain that comedy is one of those activities and I would not oppose condemning it with the rest. But if indeed there are intervals between acts of piety, and if men need distraction, I believe that one cannot find one that would be more innocent than comedy. I have said too much. Let us end with a word about *Tartuffe* spoken by a great prince.

Eight days after it was banned, actors presented to the court a play called *Scaramouche the Hermit,* and the king, leaving the performance, said to the prince the words that I am about to report: "I would like to know why those who were so scandalized by Molière's comedy say nothing about *Scaramouche.*" To which the prince replied: "The reason is that the comedy of *Scaramouche* mocks Heaven and religion, which those gentlemen do not care about, but Molière's play mocks those gentlemen themselves, and they cannot endure that."

Tartuffe

Cast of Characters[2]

Mme. Pernelle, mother of Orgon
Orgon, husband of Elmire
Elmire, wife of Orgon
Damis, son of Orgon
Mariane, daughter of Orgon and beloved of Valère
Valère, beloved of Mariane
Cléante, brother-in-law of Orgon and brother of Elmire
Tartuffe, a hypocrite
Dorine, maid and confidante of Mariane
M. Loyal, a beadle
an Officer of the court
Flipote, maidservant of Mme. Pernelle

The play takes place in Paris.

---

2. See the note on the names of characters on pages 119–21.

Act I

Scene 1

MME. PERNELLE, FLIPOTE, ELMIRE,
DORINE, DAMIS, CLÉANTE, MARIANE

Mme. Pernelle
Come on, Flipote, come on, so I can get away.

Elmire
You walk so fast: it's hard to keep up with you.

Mme. Pernelle
Stay where you are, Daughter-in-Law—don't come any farther. I don't need manners like yours.

Elmire
We have behaved properly, Mother; why are you leaving so quickly?

Mme. Pernelle
I cannot stand the way this household is run. No one ever makes any effort to please me. Yes, I am leaving. I've seen

some shocking behavior: my instructions are rejected; no one respects me; everyone speaks arrogantly—it's Bedlam here.

Dorine
If . . .

Mme. Pernelle
You, Miss, are a chatterbox, not a proper lady's companion, and a rude one too, who insists on sharing your opinions about everything.

Damis
But . . .

Mme. Pernelle
You are a four-letter . . . fool. I'm your grandmother and I should know. I've told your father a hundred times that you act like a good-for-nothing and that you'll never be more than a nuisance to him.

Mariane
I think . . .

Mme. Pernelle
Now, now, Mademoiselle, you may act discreetly and seem meek and well behaved, but "still waters run deep," as they say. I know you're simply covering up unsavory behavior.

Elmire
But Mother . . .

Mme. Pernelle
Daughter-in-Law, your conduct, if I may say so, is perfectly shocking. You should be setting a good example for these children—which their late mother certainly did. You're extravagant; I'm horrified to see you dressed up like a princess.

Tartuffe, Act I, scene 1

A woman whose only concern is to please her husband doesn't need to wear such finery.

Cléante
But Madame, after all . . .

Mme. Pernelle
As for you, her brother, I admire you; I like you, honor you—but if I were my son, her husband, I would beg you never to set foot in this house. You're forever offering advice on how to live that no decent people should accept. I don't mince words; that's the way I am, and I don't hesitate to say what's on my mind.

Damis
Your Monsieur Tartuffe is a lucky man, no doubt . . .

Mme. Pernelle
He is a righteous man; you should listen to him. I cannot bear to see him challenged by a fool like you.

Damis
What, should I allow a bigoted hypocrite to be a tyrant in this house? Are we forbidden to enjoy ourselves unless that fine fellow deigns to permit it?

Dorine
If we're to believe what he says, we're all acting like criminals; that fanatic controls everything.

Mme. Pernelle
And he controls everything properly. He intends to lead you to Heaven, and my son is right to urge you to love him.

Damis
No—look here, Grandmother, neither Father nor anyone else can make me wish him well. I'd be a traitor to myself if I said

anything else; everything he does infuriates me. Something's going to happen; someday I'll be forced to lock horns with that lout.

Dorine
It's a scandal to see a stranger become the master here. That beggar who arrived barefoot, his clothes in tatters—well, now he forgets who he is, contradicts everyone, and tells everyone what to do.

Mme. Pernelle
Good Lord! Things would go better if everyone followed his pious example.

Dorine
You imagine that he's a saint; well, believe me, he's only a hypocrite.

Mme. Pernelle
Watch your tongue!

Dorine
Me, I wouldn't trust him or his servant Laurent unless I had a solid guarantee.

Mme. Pernelle
I don't in fact know about the servant, but I'll guarantee that the master is a righteous man. The only reason you wish him ill and defy him is because he tells you the truth. Sin infuriates him; it's the wishes of Heaven that drive him.

Dorine
Oh, to be sure . . . And why did he recently forbid us to admit visitors? Does an innocent guest offend Heaven? What's the reason for all this uproar? Shall I tell you what I think? I think, to tell the truth, he's jealous of Madame.

Tartuffe, Act I, scene 1

Mme. Pernelle
Stop that! Watch what you are saying. He's not the only one to criticize these visits. All the commotion that those people make, all those carriages parked in front of the door, all those servants making a hubbub in the neighborhood . . . I'd like to think that nothing scandalous is happening, but people do talk, and that's bad.

Cléante
Come, come, Madame, can one possibly stop such talk? It would be a shame if we had to abandon our friends because of silly gossip—and even if we did, do you think we could silence those folks? There's no defense against slander. Let's pay no attention to their cackling; we'll try to live virtuously and let busybodies have their say.

Dorine
Our neighbor Daphne and that little husband of hers—aren't they the ones who talk about us so maliciously? It's always the most ridiculous people who are the first to slander others. They never miss a chance to point out the slightest hint of a romance, and happily spread the word far and wide, putting their own slant on stories that they want others to believe. They color the facts, insisting they are true, and hope—in vain, of course—that their own intrigues will seem as innocent as others' really are or that they can tar their neighbors with the same brush.

Mme. Pernelle
That's beside the point. Take [our neighbor] Orante: she leads an exemplary life; she cares only for heavenly rewards—and I have heard that she thoroughly disapproves of the things that go on here.

Dorine
An admirable example—a worthy woman! Yes, she lives austerely, but she's prudish only because she's an old lady,

and straitlaced because she has a feeble body. When she was attractive she made the most of it—now she turns her back on the world that's left her behind. All that pompous morality is just a disguise to hide her worn-out looks. That's what they do, those aging flirts who hate to see their suitors abandon them. Once they're deserted all they can do is to play the prude. Those righteous women censure everything, pardon nothing, scold everyone loudly—out of envy, not pious concern—and won't allow anyone else to enjoy the pleasures that age has denied them.

Mme. Pernelle
Those are the kinds of fairy tales you tell yourself so you can feel comfortable. Daughter-in-Law, in your house you hold the floor all the time, and we're not allowed to speak. Well, now it's my turn to talk, and I'm telling you that the wisest thing my son ever did was to welcome this virtuous man into his home. Heaven sent him here because someone had to bring your lost souls back to the right path. You should listen to him for your own good; he rebukes what needs to be reformed. These visits, balls, and evenings of chitchat are all inventions of the devil. I've never heard a pious word exchanged; it's all idle talk, foolishness, gossip about the neighbors, slanders, backbiting, a thousand false reports based on absolutely nothing. Honest folks' heads are spinning with all this confusion; no wonder that the other day a wise man called it a second tower of Babylon. Everyone babbles on and on and on. I'll tell you the story that provoked this comment—right—this gentleman [*Pointing to Cléante.*][1] is snickering already! Right, you'll have to look elsewhere for the fools who can make you laugh, and without . . . Good-bye, Daughter-in-Law, I don't want to say another word. You should know that I've told only half the story—and it will be a long time before I set foot in here again.

---

1. The italicized notes in brackets are stage directions that date from the first performances of *Tartuffe*.

Tartuffe, Act I, scene 1

[*She slaps Flipote.*] Come on, don't stand there gaping! Just wait! I'll give you something to listen to. Come on, Slip-Slop, come along.

Scene 2

Cléante, Dorine

Cléante
I don't want to leave yet; I'm afraid she'll continue to scold me. May that old lady . . .

Dorine
A pity she didn't hear you say that! She'd say, "Thank you very much" for the compliment and that she's not old enough to deserve it.

Cléante
She gets angry with us about nothing, and she seems to be besotted by her Tartuffe.

Dorine
She's nothing compared to her son. If you'd seen him, you'd have said, "He's much worse!" In the recent "troubles" he was known as a level-headed man who backed his king courageously.[2] But he's become a blockhead since he became infatuated with Tartuffe. He calls him brother, loves him a hundred times more than his own mother, son, daughter, wife. He tells Tartuffe all his secrets; he treats Tartuffe like his confessor, who judges his acts. He cherishes Tartuffe,

---

2. See the note on this sentence on pages 121–22.

embraces him; he couldn't love a mistress more tenderly. He makes Tartuffe sit next to him at dinner—happily watches him eat enough for six people, makes everyone give him the best bits, and when Tartuffe belches, says, "God bless you." [*This is a servant speaking.*] Orgon is crazy about him, thinks the world of him, quotes everything he says as if it were gospel, and Tartuffe, who knows his dupe and how to play him, bamboozles him with a hundred sanctimonious tricks. His hypocrisy has made him rich and entitles him to criticize everything we do. Even his stupid servant makes it his business to tell us how to behave, preaching wildly at us and throwing out our ribbons and our makeup. That fiend snatched away—with his own hands—a bit of lace that he found pressed flat in *The Lives of the Saints* because, said he, we were polluting holy writings with the devil's finery.

Scene 3

ELMIRE, MARIANE, DAMIS,
CLÉANTE, DORINE

Elmire
You're lucky that you weren't at the speech that she [Mme. Pernelle] gave as she was leaving. — I've just seen my husband; since he didn't see me, I'll go upstairs to wait for him.

Cléante
I'll wait for him here so that I don't waste time; I'll just say hello.

Damis
Say something to him about my sister's marriage; I suspect that Tartuffe opposes it, since he forces my father to delay it so much. You know that I take a special interest in all this. If my sister and Valère love each other, well, Valère's sister is very dear to me, and if it were necessary . . .

Dorine
Here he comes.

Scene 4

Orgon, Cléante, Dorine

Orgon [*To Cléante.*]
Hello there, Brother.

Cléante
I was just leaving, and I'm delighted to see you. The countryside isn't much in bloom just yet.

Orgon
Dorine . . . Brother-in-Law, wait a moment, please; just let me reassure myself by hearing all the news . . . Has all gone well these past two days? What's happened? Is everyone well?

Dorine
Madame's had a fever until the day before yesterday in the evening, with a terrible headache.

Orgon
And Tartuffe?

Dorine
Tartuffe? He couldn't be better: fat, happy, his complexion is good, his lips are rosy.

Tartuffe, Act I, scene 4

Orgon
The poor fellow!

Dorine
Last evening she had no appetite and couldn't eat any supper because her headache was so bad.

Orgon
And Tartuffe?

Dorine
He was the only one who ate—while she watched—and he piously consumed two partridges and half a leg of chopped lamb.

Orgon
The poor fellow!

Dorine
She scarcely closed her eyes all night; fevers kept her from sleeping, and we had to watch her closely until dawn.

Orgon
And Tartuffe?

Dorine
He grew pleasantly drowsy as soon as he left the dining table, went to his room and hopped quickly into his nice warm bed, where he slept until morning.

Orgon
The poor fellow!

Dorine
Finally she agreed to be bled and immediately felt better.

Orgon
And Tartuffe?

Dorine
He was very brave, and he drank four large glasses of wine to strengthen his soul against harm and to rebuild the blood that Madame had lost.

Orgon
The poor fellow!

Dorine
Both are doing well, and I'll go tell Madame how encouraged you are by her convalescence.

Scene 5

ORGON, CLÉANTE

Cléante
Brother, she's laughing in your face. I don't want to upset you, but I must say she's right. Who ever heard of such foolishness? How can he charm you enough to make you forget everything except for him? He has recovered from his troubles since he's been living here, and now you have come to the point that . . .

Orgon
Stop, Brother-in-Law. You don't know the man you're talking about.

Cléante
Well, perhaps I don't know him, but to recognize what kind of a man he may be . . .

Orgon
My brother, you would be delighted to know him, and your admiration would be endless. He's a man who . . . hmm . . . a man, well then, a man. Anyone who takes his teaching seriously feels profound peace, looks at the world as if it were only a dunghill. Yes, I become a changed man when I listen to him. He teaches me to love nothing in this world, he frees my soul from all affection, and I could watch my brother, children, mother, wife die without the least concern.

Tartuffe, Act I, scene 5

Cléante
What humane emotions those are, dear brother!

Orgon
Oh, if you had known how I first met him, you would have had the same affection for him that I have. He came to church every day, knelt near me, looking so humble. Everyone noticed how fervently he prayed, sighed, groaned, how often he kissed the ground; and when I left the church, he hurried ahead of me to offer holy water. I learned about his poverty and his origins from his servant, who imitated him in everything; I gave him alms, but he modestly insisted on returning some of what I had given him. "It's too much," he said, "too much by half; I'm not worthy of your compassion." And when I refused to take any back, he rushed — right then and there — to give it to the poor. At last Heaven allowed him to come to live here, and since then all seems to be well. He looks better and even pays very special attention to my wife, warning me about those who flirt with her; he's six times more jealous than I am. And you wouldn't believe how high-minded he is: he calls the least little thing sinful; a mere nothing scandalizes him — to the point that the other day he condemned himself for having caught a louse while he was praying and squeezing it to death too angrily.

Cléante
Good grief, Brother, you seem to me to have gone mad. Are you making fun of me? And do you really think that this silliness . . .

Orgon
Brother, this kind of comment smells like impiety to me. Your soul is beginning to be corrupted; I've told you at least ten times that you are in spiritual danger.

Cléante
People like you always say things like that. They want

everyone to be as blind as they are. They think that seeing clearly is impiety, that those who refuse to worship false idols have no respect for true faith and true religion. Such talk doesn't frighten me; I know what I'm saying, and Heaven itself knows what I think. I'm not a slave to fraud. Look: some people pretend to be religious the way others pretend to be brave. We can recognize brave people by what honor has pushed them to do, but the truly pious, whom one should imitate, don't smirk and show off. Come on! Can't you tell the difference between hypocrisy and true piety? You treat them as if they were identical; you respect a mask as if it were a real face. Do you think that pretense and sincerity, appearance and truth, phantom and reality, counterfeit and real currency are all the same? What strange creatures men are! They're always off balance; they think being reasonable is too limiting; they spoil what's best by pushing things too far.—All this is just a casual observation, dear brother-in-law.

Orgon
Oh yes, without a doubt you're a revered professor who embodies all the wisdom of the world, the only truly wise and enlightened man, an oracle, a Cato[3] in our generation; compared with you, of course, all other men are fools.

Cléante
Brother, I'm not a revered professor; I don't embody all the world's wisdom. What I do know is how to distinguish between true and false. I don't know any heroes more worthy of respect than the truly pious or anything more noble and beautiful than holy passion and saintly zeal. And I don't know anything more hateful than those whited sepulchres, the phony zealots, the obvious charlatans with their ostentatious

---

3. Cato (234–149 BCE)—a distinguished lawyer, soldier, legislator, and ambassador—was considered a model of morality both in his day and in later generations; his name became a synonym for civic and personal virtue.

piety, their sacrilegious and deceitful behavior, who brazenly
take advantage of others, who distort, whenever they please,
what we human beings think is most saintly and sacred.
They dedicate their souls only to their own interests; for
them, religion is a business, or merchandise, and they try to
buy honor and position by deceptive winks and exaggerated
enthusiasm. I'm talking about those sanctimonious fellows
who use religious zeal to fatten their bank accounts, who
attach themselves to the Court while preaching austerity,
who adjust their piety to fit their vices. They're treacherous,
hasty, vindictive, full of tricks; they hide their envy and claim
that their desire to ruin others is God's will. Their hostility
and fanaticism—much good may it do them—are all the more
dangerous because they use our own holy weapons against us.
We see these liars all too often, and yet it's easy to recognize
those who are truly devout. There are splendid examples
these days, dear brother: look at Ariston, Périandre, Oronte,
Alcidamas, Polydore, Clitandre—no one doubts what they are.
They don't parade their virtue; they're not ostentatious; their
piety is on a human scale—it's sober, well balanced. They're
not constantly censuring what we do: they think it's arrogance
to condemn others. They let others speak angrily; meanwhile
their behavior silently corrects ours. Though they're not
impressed by appearances, their instinct is to think well of
others. No cabals, no intrigues: their chief concern is to live
properly. They don't attack sinners, though they hate the sin.
They don't confuse Heaven's will with their own zeal. These
are the ones I admire; this is how one should behave; this is
the model to imitate. Your fellow isn't like that. You praise his
zeal in good faith; well, I'm afraid you've been dazzled by his
pretentious behavior.

Orgon
Brother-in-Law, have you said all you want to say?

Cléante
Yes.

Orgon
Your servant, sir. [*He starts to leave.*]

Cléante
One more word, Brother. Let's turn to something else. You know that Valère has asked to marry your daughter?

Orgon
Yes.

Cléante
You had fixed a date for the wedding.

Orgon
True.

Cléante
Why have you delayed it?

Orgon
I don't know.

Cléante
Have you some other plan?

Orgon
Perhaps.

Cléante
You would break your word?

Orgon
I wouldn't put it that way.

Tartuffe, Act I, scene 5

Cléante
There's no obstacle, I imagine, to keeping your promise.

Orgon
As you say.

Cléante
Is it so difficult to go ahead with it? Valère asked me to speak to you about it.

Orgon
Heaven be praised!

Cléante
But what shall I tell him?

Orgon
Whatever you like.

Cléante
But we need to know your plans. What are they?

Orgon
To do as Heaven demands.

Cléante
Let's talk frankly. Valère has your promise; will you keep it or not?

Orgon
Good-bye.

Cléante
I feel uneasy about the prospects for Valère's happiness; I'd better warn him about what has happened.

Act II

Scene 1

ORGON, MARIANE

Orgon
Mariane.

Mariane
Father.

Orgon
Come a bit closer. I have something to say to you privately.

Mariane
What are you looking for?

Orgon [*He looks in a little closet.*]
I'm making sure that no one can overhear us; this little closet could hold an eavesdropper. Fine: all's well. Mariane, I've always known that you have a gentle soul, and you have always been very dear to me.

Tartuffe, Act II, scene 1

Mariane
I'm deeply grateful for your fatherly love.

Orgon
Well said, Daughter, and if you want that love to continue, all you have to think about is pleasing me.

Mariane
It's my pleasure to please you.

Orgon
Quite right. Now, what do you think of our guest Tartuffe?

Mariane
Who, me?

Orgon
Yes, you. Be careful what you say.

Mariane
Oh goodness, I'll say anything you like.

Orgon
Well said. Now, Daughter, say that his good works shine through him everywhere, that he touches your heart, and that you would be delighted if I chose him for your husband. Well?

Mariane [*She jumps back in surprise.*]
Well?

Orgon
What's the matter?

Mariane
I beg your pardon?

Tartuffe, Act II, scene 1

Orgon
What?

Mariane
Did I misunderstand?

Orgon
Misunderstand?

Mariane
What do you want me to say, Father? Who has touched my heart? That I would be pleased if you chose whom as my husband?

Orgon
Tartuffe.

Mariane
Not at all, Father—none of that is true. Why do you ask me to invent something untrue?

Orgon
But I want it to be true. You should be satisfied with what I have decided.

Mariane
What? You want, Father . . .

Orgon
Yes, Daughter, I intend to join Tartuffe and our family in marriage. He will be your husband, I've decided that, and since your wishes . . .

Scene 2

Dorine, Orgon, Mariane

Orgon [*To Dorine.*]
What are you doing there? Are you so curious, Miss, that you have come to listen to us?

Dorine
So curious, Monsieur, that I can't believe what you have said.

Orgon
I know how to make you believe it.

Dorine
Oh yes, you're telling us a joke.

Orgon
Just wait and see.

Dorine
Fiddlesticks!

Orgon
Daughter, I am not joking.

Dorine
Come on, don't believe Monsieur your father; he's teasing.

Tartuffe, Act II, scene 2

Orgon
I tell you . . .

Dorine
No, say what you will, no one will believe you.

Orgon
I'm growing very angry . . .

Dorine
Very well, then, we believe you, and so much the worse for you. Come on, Monsieur, with all those fine whiskers in the middle of your face, you look like a wise man; can it be that you are crazy enough to want . . .

Orgon
Listen here! You're being very impertinent. I don't like that; I'm warning you, Miss.

Dorine
Let's not become angry, Monsieur. Are you making fun of us with this plot? A religious fanatic doesn't need a girl; he should be thinking about other things. Moreover, what advantage to you would such a marriage be? You're well-to-do; why choose a beggar for a son-in-law?

Orgon
Be quiet! If he is a beggar, all the more reason to respect him. His poverty is no disgrace; it's more honorable than any worldly titles. After all—as you know—he was poor because he was intensely spiritual and didn't pay enough attention to earthly matters. Well, my support will help him get out of his difficulties and regain his property, which is highly regarded in his part of the country. As anyone can see, he comes from a very good family.

Tartuffe, Act II, scene 2

Dorine
Yes, he says so himself. Is vanity like that really a sign of piety? Someone who embraces an innocent and holy life shouldn't boast about his family; humility and devotion don't go along with ambition like his. What is the point of this pride? . . . Oh, these comments upset you? Let's talk about him as a person and not as a nobleman. Do you think it's a good idea to give a young woman like your daughter to a man like that? Think about what's appropriate; can't you foresee the consequences of such a marriage? Be careful: a young woman's virtue is in danger if she's married off to someone she doesn't want. Her willingness to live an honorable life depends on the character of the husband she's been given. Men who behave badly force their wives to do the same. It's very difficult, I must say, to be faithful to certain kinds of husbands. Someone who gives his daughter to a man she hates becomes responsible for her sins. Think of the dangers you face with a plan like this.

Orgon
What! Am I supposed to learn how to live from her?

Dorine
You cannot do better than follow my instructions.

Orgon
Let's not distract ourselves with nonsense. [*To Mariane.*] I know what you need, and I am your father. Yes, I did promise you to Valère. Now, in addition to the fact that people say he gambles, I suspect he's something of a freethinker. I haven't seen him in church very often.

Dorine
Do you want him to go there on a schedule, like the people who go only to be noticed?

Tartuffe, Act II, scene 2

Orgon
I'm not asking for your opinion. Tartuffe is in Heaven's good graces, and that is the best kind of wealth. [*To Mariane.*] This fine marriage will give you everything you want; you'll have nothing but sweetness and pleasure. You'll live together, joined by faithful love, like two dear children, two turtledoves. You'll never quarrel, and you can make of him whatever you might wish.

Dorine
All she'll be able to make of him is a fool.

Orgon
What kind of a thing is that to say!

Dorine
I tell you that he's born under the sign of the fool, and the alignment of his stars will trump all your daughter's virtues.

Orgon
Stop interrupting me! Be quiet! Stop poking your nose into other people's business.

Dorine
I'm only trying to help you. [*She interrupts him each time he turns to talk to his daughter.*]

Orgon
Don't trouble yourself on my account; just be quiet.

Dorine
If I didn't care for you . . .

Orgon
I don't want you to care for me.

Tartuffe, Act II, scene 2

Dorine
I want to care for you, despite yourself.

Orgon
Oh!

Dorine
Your honor is important to me. I can't bear to see you become the butt of other people's jokes.

Orgon
Will you never be still?

Dorine
It would be unconscionable to let you make such a marriage.

Orgon
Will you stop talking, you viper, you outrageous . . .

Dorine
Oh, you're so pious, but you still lose your temper?

Orgon
Yes, I do. Listening to this stupidity makes me feel sick. I insist that you hold your tongue.

Dorine
Very well. But even if I don't speak, I'm thinking.

Orgon
Think if you must, but keep it to yourself, or . . . That's enough. [*Turning to Mariane.*] As a wise man, I have thought soberly about everything.

Dorine
I'm furious that I'm not allowed to speak. [*She stops speaking as Orgon turns his head.*]

Tartuffe, Act II, scene 2

Orgon
Though Tartuffe isn't a fashion plate, he's . . .

Dorine
Oh yes, he's cute enough.

Orgon
. . . personable, so that even if you don't relish all his other abilities . . . [*He turns toward Dorine and looks at her, his arms folded.*]

Dorine
There's a lucky girl! If I were in her shoes, no man would force me to marry, and if it happened, I'd show him soon enough that a woman always has her revenge prepared.

Orgon
So, no one pays attention to what I have said?

Dorine
Why are you complaining? I wasn't talking to you.

Orgon
Then what were you doing?

Dorine
I was talking to myself.

Orgon
Right. The back of my hand will teach you something. [*He prepares to slap Dorine, and each time he looks at her, Dorine stands still without talking.*] Daughter, it is your duty to accept my plan. Please believe that the husband I have chosen for you . . . [*To Dorine.*] What? You're not saying anything?

Dorine
I have nothing to tell myself.

Orgon
Just one word.

Dorine
I don't want to.

Orgon
I was watching you.

Dorine
My word, what a fool!

Orgon [*To Mariane.*]
Daughter, do your duty and defer to my choice.

Dorine [*Running away.*]
I'd be laughed at if I accepted such a husband. [*Orgon tries to slap her and misses.*]

Orgon
That girl of yours, dear daughter, is worse than the plague. If I had to put up with her, I don't know what I'd . . . I'm in no condition to go on; her insolence drives me wild. I'm going out for a walk to calm down.

Scene 3

DORINE, MARIANE

Dorine
Have you lost your tongue; do I have to do all the talking for you? To put up with such an insane proposal without saying a word!

Mariane
With a tyrant for a father, what can I do?

Dorine
Whatever you can to ward off this disaster.

Mariane
Such as what?

Dorine
Tell him that hearts don't fall in love at someone else's command; that you marry to please yourself, not him; that since you are the one who is involved, you are the one whom the husband has to please—and if he loves his Tartuffe so much, he should marry him.

Mariane
But a father has so much power over us that I've never had the strength to say anything.

Dorine
Let's be serious. Valère has courted you; do you love him or don't you?

Mariane
You are unfair to me. How can you doubt my love? Haven't I told you a hundred times how I feel about him, how much I love him?

Dorine
Who knows whether that's your mouth or your heart speaking. Then you really do love him?

Mariane
You're wrong to doubt me; I've shown my feelings all too clearly.

Dorine
Well—do you really love him?

Mariane
Yes, passionately.

Dorine
And as far as one can tell, he loves you too?

Mariane
I believe he does.

Dorine
And both of you are desperate to marry each other?

Mariane
Certainly.

Dorine
Then what do you think of this other proposal?

Tartuffe, Act II, scene 3

Mariane
If I'm forced to do that, I'll kill myself.

Dorine
Right: that's a remedy I hadn't thought of. All you have to do to get out of this difficulty is to die. A wonderful remedy. That kind of talk infuriates me.

Mariane
Good grief! What a temper you're in! You don't seem to have any sympathy with other people's unhappiness.

Dorine
I have no sympathy for people like you who talk nonsense and tremble when they face difficulties.

Mariane
But what can I do? I'm easily frightened.

Dorine
Lovers must be brave.

Mariane
But don't I still love Valère? Isn't he the one who must ask for my hand?

Dorine
Come on, even if your father is a stubborn fool, enamored of his Tartuffe, determined to break the marriage contract that he agreed to—is that your lover's fault?

Mariane
But if I reject my father's choice out of hand, if I show my disgust, wouldn't I also show my feelings too much? If I let others know how much Valère dazzles me, wouldn't I be abandoning proper womanly modesty and my duties as a daughter? Do you want my passion broadcast . . .

Tartuffe, Act II, scene 3

Dorine
No, no—I don't want anything. I see that you want to belong to Monsieur Tartuffe, and when I think about it, I see that I'm wrong to deter you from this marriage. What reason is there to oppose your wishes? In himself, he's such a good catch. Monsieur Tartuffe! Well, well! You're not being offered a nobody. In fact, Monsieur Tartuffe isn't a buffoon; it's a bit of luck to become his better half. Everyone already honors him. At home he's a nobleman—handsome, red ears, and ruddy complexion—you'd live a very happy life with such a husband.

Mariane
My God! . . .

Dorine
What joy you'll feel when you find yourself the wife of such a fine man!

Mariane
Oh, please stop talking that way, and show me how to rescue myself from this marriage. That's it. I give up; I'm ready to do anything.

Dorine
No, a daughter must obey her father, even though he wants to marry her to an ape. You're a lucky girl; why are you complaining? You'll go in a wagon to his little town, which you'll find full of uncles and cousins whom you'll be happy to entertain. First of all, they'll make you visit the best families. You'll be welcomed by the wife of the bailiff and the tax collector; they'll honor you by offering you a folding chair. At carnival time you can expect to go to a ball where you'll be entertained by two bagpipes, a trained monkey, and a puppet show—that is, if your husband . . .

Mariane
Oh, you're killing me. Give me some advice that will help me.

Dorine
I'm your servant, Miss.

Mariane
Dorine, please . . .

Dorine
You'll just have to put up with this marriage.

Mariane
My dear . . .

Dorine
No.

Mariane
If my wishes, which I've told you . . .

Dorine
Not at all. Tartuffe is the man for you, as you'll soon find out.

Mariane
You know I've always confided in you and trusted you. Please . . .

Dorine
No, indeed. I promise: you'll be thoroughly Tartuffified.

Mariane
Well, since you're not sympathetic to my troubles, leave me alone with my despair, which will steady my heart. I know the infallible cure for my troubles. [*She starts to leave.*]

Dorine
Wait! Come on, come back. I've stopped being difficult. Despite it all, I do have pity on you.

Mariane
Can't you see? If I am condemned to be tortured, I tell you, Dorine, I'm better off dead.

Dorine
Don't worry; we can prevent it quite cleverly . . . But look, here's your beloved Valère.

Scene 4

Valère, Mariane, Dorine

Valère
I've just had some news, Madame, that I did not know and that must surely be good.

Mariane
What is that?

Valère
That you are to marry Tartuffe.

Mariane
Well, my father certainly has this plan in mind.

Valère
Your father, Madame . . .

Mariane
Has changed his mind; he has only just presented this idea to me.

Valère
What? Seriously?

Mariane
Yes, seriously. He has publicly announced that he wants this marriage.

Tartuffe, Act II, scene 4

Valère
And what do you think about this, Madame?

Mariane
I don't know.

Valère
A truthful answer. You don't know?

Mariane
No.

Valère
No?

Mariane
What do you advise?

Valère
Me? I advise you to accept this husband.

Mariane
That's what you advise?

Valère
Yes.

Mariane
Really and truly?

Valère
Without doubt: it's a prestigious match, worth paying attention to.

Mariane
Well, then, Sir, I accept your advice.

Valère
You won't have any difficulty taking it, I suppose.

Mariane
No more than you had in giving it.

Valère
Me? I gave you that advice to please you.

Mariane
Then I will take it to please you.

Dorine
Let's see what comes of all this.

Valère
Is this what love means? Were you deceiving me when you . . .

Mariane
Please, let's not talk about this any more. You told me bluntly that I must accept the husband who has been chosen for me, and I intend to do it, since you give me such helpful advice.

Valère
Don't blame me: you had already made a decision, and you are using a very feeble excuse to break your word.

Mariane
Oh yes, well said.

Valère
Indeed. And you never truly loved me.

Mariane
Alas . . . you may think so if you wish.

Valère
Yes, yes, if I wish. But I've been hurt, and that may push me to act before you do; I know how to change my mind and to whom to offer my hand.

Mariane
Oh, I don't doubt it, and merit excites passion . . .

Valère
Forget about merit: I clearly have very little, as you have just demonstrated. But I'm sure that others might be kind to me and would happily compensate me for my loss when they learn that I've been dismissed.

Mariane
You haven't lost much, and you'll easily comfort yourself in this changed situation.

Valère
I'll do my best, you may be sure. When your self-respect is hurt, when you're abandoned, then you ought to forget the person who hurt you. Even if you fail, you have to pretend you've succeeded. No one forgives the coward who continues to love someone who doesn't want him.

Mariane
What a lofty and noble sentiment.

Valère
Yes indeed, and everyone will certainly agree with it. What — do you want me to keep on loving you forever? Do you want me to watch you in someone else's arms and not look for someone who would welcome the heart you rejected?

Mariane
Not at all. It's the very thing I hoped for; I wish it were already done.

Valère
You do?

Mariane
Yes.

Valère
You have insulted me enough, Madame; I'll leave and make you happy. [*He takes a few steps and then turns back.*]

Mariane
Fine.

Valère
Please remember that you're forcing me to do this.

Mariane
Yes.

Valère
And my intentions simply imitate your own.

Mariane
My own. Very well.

Valère
Fine. You'll find yourself obeyed.

Mariane
All the better.

Valère
You have seen the last of me.

Mariane
Good enough.

Valère
Oh? [*He leaves and when he reaches the door turns back.*]

Mariane
Yes?

Valère
Did you call?

Mariane
I? You must be dreaming.

Valère
Ah, well then, I'll keep going. Good-bye, Madame.

Mariane
Good-bye, Monsieur.

Dorine
This foolishness makes me think you both have lost your wits. I've let you quarrel to see what would happen. Holà! Seigneur Valère. [*She holds his arm, and he pretends to resist.*]

Valère
Hey! What are you doing, Dorine?

Dorine
Come here.

Valère
No, I'm too angry; don't interfere with what she's forcing me to do.

Dorine
Stop.

Valère
No. Can't you see I have made up my mind?

Dorine
Oh!

Mariane
Seeing me hurts him; my being here drives him away. I'd better leave.

Dorine [*She leaves Valère and runs to Mariane.*]
Here's the other one. Where are you running to?

Mariane
Leave me alone.

Dorine
You have to come back.

Mariane
No, no, Dorine, holding me here is useless.

Valère
I see that the very sight of me is torture for her; it would be better to relieve her pain.

Dorine [*She leaves Mariane and runs to Valère.*]
You again? Devil take me if I let this happen. Stop these games, and come here, both of you. [*She pulls them together.*]

Valère
What are you up to?

Mariane
What are you trying to do?

Dorine
Put the two of you back together, pull you out of this mess. Are you crazy to be squabbling like this?

Valère
Didn't you hear how she was speaking to me?

Dorine [*To Mariane.*]
Are you crazy to have lost your temper this way?

Mariane
Didn't you see how he treated me?

Dorine
Double craziness. All she cares about is keeping you—I can testify to that. He loves only you, and the only thing he wants is to marry you—I swear it.

Mariane [*To Valère.*]
Then why did you give me that advice?

Valère [*To Mariane.*]
Why did you ask for advice on such a subject?

Dorine
You are both crazy. Here—give me your hand. Come on, you.

Valère [*Giving his hand to Dorine.*]
Why do you want it?

Dorine
Ah! Now yours.

Mariane [*Giving her hand to Dorine.*]
What's all this for?

Tartuffe, Act II, scene 4

Dorine
Hurry up; come here. You love each other more than you think.

Valère
Don't be so difficult; stop looking at people so angrily. [*Mariane looks sideways at Valère and smiles a little.*]

Dorine
I must say, all lovers are crazy.

Valère
Ho! Don't I have a right to complain about you? Tell the truth: weren't you wicked to enjoy telling me such terrible things?

Mariane
And you, aren't you the most ungrateful man . . .

Dorine
Let's leave such talk for some other time. Right now we must think about preventing this dreadful marriage.

Mariane
Tell us how to do it.

Dorine
We'll do everything we can. Your father is being a fool, talking nonsense. But it would be best for the two of you to pretend you agree to his foolish ideas. That way, it will be easier for you to delay this proposed marriage if you have to. Once we have time, we can do anything. You could suddenly have a terrible illness, which will mean postponing the wedding, or you will have had a terrifying nightmare that foretells disaster. Maybe you saw a dead man or broke a mirror or dreamed of a swamp. In any case, no one can force you to marry anyone unless you say "yes." Now, I think it would be better if you two were not

seen talking together. [*To Valère.*] Leave, and urge your friends to help you get what was promised to you. We'll go and warn Orgon's brother-in-law and enlist Elmire's help.

Valère [*To Mariane.*]
Whatever else is done, you are my chief source of hope.

Mariane [*To Valère.*]
I can't be responsible for a father's wishes, but I will not give myself to anyone other than to you.

Valère
You fill me with joy! And though I dare . . .

Dorine
Oh, lovers! They never stop chattering. Leave, I tell you.

Valère [*He takes a step and turns back.*]
Well . . .

Dorine
What's all this jibber-jabber? You, go this way. And you—the other. [*She pushes them by the shoulders.*]

Act III

Scene 1

DAMIS, DORINE

Damis
All right! Come on, lightning, strike me! Or maybe I should just bash my head against the wall! Don't try to stop me—I'm no fool!

Dorine
Calm down: all your father did was talk about it. Not everything that's proposed is done—there's a long way between starting a plan and finishing it.

Damis
I've got to stop that upstart in his tracks and tell him a thing or two.

Dorine
Slow down! Let Elmire help you with your father and that fellow. She's got some influence over Tartuffe. He agrees with everything she says; for all I know he's a little bit in love with her. Let's hope so! That would be a great help. After all this

Tartuffe, Act III, scene 1

fuss she'll have to send for Tartuffe so she can find out what he thinks of this marriage that disturbs you so much and warn him that if he encourages these plans, there will be unpleasant consequences. I haven't been able to see him; his valet says he's praying and that he'll be coming here soon. So leave, please, and let me wait for him.

Damis
I could stay for the whole conversation.

Dorine
Certainly not. They must be alone together.

Damis
I won't say a word to him.

Dorine
Don't be silly; I know how excitable you are—you'd just spoil everything. Leave.

Damis
No. I want to watch. I promise I won't become angry.

Dorine
What a nuisance you are. Here he comes! Go away. [*Damis hides.*]

Scene 2

TARTUFFE, DORINE

Tartuffe [*Seeing Dorine.*]
Laurent, put away my hair shirt and my lash, and pray constantly for Heaven's instruction.[4] If someone comes to see me, say that I have gone to visit those in prison, to distribute the little alms money that I have.

Dorine
What an affected show-off!

Tartuffe
What do you want?

Dorine
To tell you . . .

Tartuffe [*He pulls a handkerchief from his pocket.*]
O Heaven! I beg you, take this handkerchief before you say another word.

Dorine
What?

---

4. See the note on this sentence on pages 122–24.

Tartuffe, Act III, scene 2

Tartuffe
Cover your bosom, which I may not see. Souls are harmed and sinful thoughts are generated by such sights.

Dorine
Are you tempted that easily? Are you so preoccupied by the flesh? How come you're so hot? I'm not aroused that quickly; I could see you stark naked from head to toe without being the least bit tempted.

Tartuffe
A bit more modesty in your speech, Miss, or I shall leave immediately.

Dorine
No, no, I'll leave you alone; I only have a couple of words to tell you. Madame is coming down here and begs you to allow her to speak to you for a moment.

Tartuffe
Aha! Yes, very willingly.

Dorine [*To herself.*]
He mellows pretty quickly! I think my suspicions were right.

Tartuffe
Will she come soon?

Dorine
I think I hear her—yes, here she is in person; I'll leave you two together.

Scene 3

Elmire, Tartuffe

Tartuffe
May Heaven in all its mercy assure your health in soul and body, and may it bless your days. This is the wish of the most humble of those inspired by sacred love.

Elmire
Thank you for those pious wishes. Now, let's sit down and be a bit more comfortable.

Tartuffe
Are you feeling somewhat better after your illness?

Elmire
Much better; the fever has broken.

Tartuffe
My own prayers do not have enough merit to attract Heaven's mercy, but I have not ceased praying for your return to health.

Elmire
Such zeal was unnecessary.

Tartuffe
No one can pray too much for your well-being; I would gladly give my own health for yours.

Elmire
That's pushing Christian charity very far; I thank you for your kindness.

Tartuffe
I do far less for you than you deserve.

Elmire
I wanted to talk to you privately about a certain matter, and I am very glad that no one is listening.

Tartuffe
I too am delighted; how sweet it is, Madame, to be alone with you. I have prayed many times for such an opportunity; only now has Heaven granted my desires.

Elmire
Well, now, I hope our conversation will let me know everything that's in your heart.

Tartuffe
And I hope only to show you my whole soul, and to assure you that I am not objecting to all your admiring visitors because of malice, but rather because of an irresistible passion and an overwhelming . . .

Elmire
I understood as much, and I know that you are concerned about my welfare.

Tartuffe [*He grasps the tips of her fingers.*]
Yes indeed, Madame, and my passion is such . . .

Elmire
Ouch! You are holding me too tightly.

Tartuffe
It is an excess of zeal, Madame. I have no intention of harming you, and indeed I would rather . . . [*He puts his hand on her knee.*]

Elmire
What is your hand doing there?

Tartuffe
I was fingering your skirt: the fabric is very soft.

Elmire
Please stop, I beg you; I am very ticklish. [*She pulls her chair back, and Tartuffe moves his forward.*]

Tartuffe
My word! What elegant embroidery! Such wonderful work is being done these days; I've never seen anything better made.

Elmire
Quite. Now, let's talk about our situation. I understand that my husband wants to break his promise and give his daughter to you. Is this true?

Tartuffe
He said a couple of words about it, but Madame, to tell the truth, this is not the happiness for which I yearn; I see elsewhere more delightful charms that would give me all the joy I desire.

Elmire
That is because worldly things don't attract you.

Tartuffe
The heart inside my bosom is not made of stone.

Elmire
Yet I think of you as devoted only to Heaven and untempted by anything here on earth.

Tartuffe, Act III, scene 3

Tartuffe
The love that draws us to eternal beauty does not stifle love of this world. Those perfect objects made by our Creator easily arouse our senses. His virtues are brilliantly reflected in yours; He has endowed you with extraordinary graces: beauty that startles the eyes and ravishes the heart. O perfect creature, I cannot see you without admiring the Author of nature, without feeling ardent love for the most beautiful portrait that He has ever painted. At first I feared that this secret passion was a clever temptation of the Evil One, and I even tried to avoid you, thinking you might be an obstacle to my salvation. But at last, most adorable beauty, I recognized that such love need not be sinful, that I could reconcile it with decency, and I surrendered to it. I dare, with great audacity, to offer you my heart, but I rely on your great kindness and not my own weak efforts. You are my hope, my good, my peace. My suffering or my salvation depends on you; your sole decree determines my happiness if you wish it, my sorrow if that is what you want.

Elmire
Such gallantry is, to tell the truth, rather surprising. You should, I think, have strengthened your heart somewhat more and thought more carefully about your intentions. A pious man like you, whom everyone calls . . .

Tartuffe
Ah! Pious one may be: one is still a man. The heart, seeing such celestial charms, is captivated and is incapable of reason. Perhaps what I have said seems unexpected, but after all, I am a man, not an angel; and if you fault this admission that I have made, blame your unearthly beauty, which provoked it. As soon as I saw it, you became the mistress of my being. Your inexpressibly sweet glances overwhelmed my stubborn heart, conquered all fasting, weeping, prayers; your beauty became the object of all my former vows. My eyes and my tears have told you this a thousand times; to explain myself

more clearly now, I must speak. If you are benevolent enough to acknowledge the suffering of your unworthy slave, if your kindness were willing to console me, to condescend to my inadequacy, I would offer, O marvel of delight, unparalleled devotion. Your reputation is not at risk; you need fear no disgrace because of me. All those men about town whom the ladies adore—they boast about their conquests and talk nonsense, they brag about their affairs and pollute the altar on which they have sacrificed their hearts. But men like me burn with hidden passion, and we keep our secrets safe; we take as good care of our reputation as we do of others'. Those who accept our hearts find love without scandal, pleasure without risk.

Elmire
I understand you; you've presented your argument quite clearly. But aren't you afraid that I might be in the mood to describe this gallant ardor to my husband and that, when he learns about the love you've described, he might want to rethink his affection for you?

Tartuffe
I know that you are infinitely kind, that you are quite willing to overlook my audacity, to forgive this human weakness, these violent expressions of a passionate love, and that you'll understand—as I see you can—that one is not blind and that a man is flesh and blood.

Elmire
Others might behave differently, of course, but I want to demonstrate my discretion. I'll say nothing of all this to my husband, but in return I ask something of you: encourage the marriage of Valère and Mariane; give up the unjust desire to enrich yourself at the expense of others and . . .

Scene 4

DAMIS, ELMIRE, TARTUFFE

Damis [*Leaving the little closet in which he had hidden.*]
No, Madame, no, this must be known. I was here; I heard everything. I think Heaven itself must have made it possible; at last I can confront the arrogant traitor who usurped my position, and take revenge for his hypocrisy and insolence. Now I can reveal him to my father and show him the soul of this double-dealer who was making love to you!

Elmire
No, Damis: all he has to do is to behave better and try to be worthy of my generosity. Don't challenge me; I made a promise. I'm not inclined to make trouble. Real women laugh at such foolishness; they don't bother to tell their husbands about it.

Damis
You may have your reasons to react this way. I have my own reasons for reacting differently. Spare him—what a joke! His hypocrisy and insolence infuriate me and have made trouble in the family. This cheat has taken advantage of my father for much too long; he has frustrated me as well as Valère. Father must be made to recognize this traitor for what he is, and Heaven has now given me a way to do that. I'm grateful to Heaven for what it has done; all this is too useful for me to

ignore. If I neglect this opportunity, I deserve to have it taken away.

Elmire
Damis . . .

Damis
No, thank you, I'll trust myself. I'm as happy as I can be; nothing you can say could persuade me to abandon the pleasures of revenge. I'm not going to wait any longer to put an end to all this; now I have just what I need to do that.

Scene 5

ORGON, DAMIS, TARTUFFE, ELMIRE

Damis [*To Orgon, who has entered.*]
We're going to delight you, Father, with news of something that has just happened that will really surprise you. All your kindness has been rewarded, and this gentleman here has repaid you handsomely. He has just demonstrated how much he respects you: by doing his best to dishonor you. I've just caught him here making scandalous propositions to Madame, who is so generous, and whose desire for discretion is so strong, that she wanted to keep this from you. Well, I can't allow his audacity to go unrecognized, and I think that failing to tell you about it is a crime.

Elmire
Well, I believe that one should not trouble one's husband with such trifles. Honor doesn't depend on reporting silliness like this; all that's necessary is to defend oneself against it: at least that's my opinion. You wouldn't have said anything, Damis, if I'd had any influence on you. [*Elmire leaves.*]

Scene 6

ORGON, DAMIS, TARTUFFE

Orgon
Oh Heavens! Can I believe my ears?

Tartuffe
Yes, my brother, I am a wicked man, a guilty one, a miserable sinner, full of vice, the worst scoundrel who ever lived. Every moment of my life has been corrupt; it is a history of crime and filth; I see now that Heaven wants to mortify me with this punishment. I will not deny committing any crime I'm accused of. Believe what you have been told; give way to your anger; drive me from your home as if I were a criminal. I would suffer less shame than I deserve.

Orgon [*To Damis.*]
You traitor! How dare you tarnish his purity with such lies?

Damis
What? Does his hypocritical confession deceive you?

Orgon
Shut up, you damned wretch.

Tartuffe
Ah! Let him speak; you are wrong to accuse him. You would do better to believe him. Why be so lenient with me? Do you

really know what I'm capable of doing? Do you trust me and think I'm a good man because of what you see? No, no, you are letting appearances deceive you; I am much less than one thinks; I am considered a righteous man, but the truth is that I am worthless. [*To Damis.*] Yes, dear son, call me a traitor, monster, sinner, thief, murderer—accuse me of even worse things; I won't contradict you. I have earned those titles, and I am willing to kneel beneath the weight of this shame, which is the result of my criminal life.

Orgon [*To Tartuffe.*]
My brother—it's too much. [*To his son.*] Will you stop now, you traitor?

Damis
What? Were his speeches so seductive that . . .

Orgon
Shut up, you good-for-nothing! [*To Tartuffe, who is kneeling.*] Dear brother, stand up, I beseech you! [*To his son.*] Brute!

Damis
He can . . .

Orgon
Shut up.

Damis
I'm going mad! What, should I . . .

Orgon
If you say one more word, I'll break your arm.

Tartuffe
In the name of God, my brother, don't let yourself be carried away. I prefer to suffer the harshest penalty rather than to have him feel the slightest scratch.

Tartuffe, Act III, scene 6

Orgon [*To his son.*]
Ingrate!

Tartuffe
Leave him in peace. If I must plead for him on both my knees...

Orgon [*To Tartuffe.*]⁵
Come—are you joking? [*To his son.*] Scoundrel! Don't you see how good he is?

Damis
Then...

Orgon
Stop!

Damis
What? I...

Orgon
Stop, I said. I know your motives for attacking him all too well. Everyone—wife, children, servants—hates and resents him. All of you are brazenly doing everything you can to take this holy man from me. But the more efforts you make to send him away, the more efforts I'll make to hold on to him. And I'll hurry to marry my daughter to him just to show up the arrogance of this family.

Damis
You'll force her to accept him?

---

5. Reports of early performances indicate that at this moment Orgon fell to his knees and embraced the kneeling Tartuffe, and that they rose as Damis began to speak.

Tartuffe, Act III, scene 6

Orgon
Yes, ingrate, and I'll do it tonight just to spite you. Ha! I defy you all; you'll see that you must obey me, that I'm the master here.⁶ Come on, apologize, you mischief-maker; kneel at his feet and ask for his forgiveness.

Damis
Who, me? From this scoundrel whose pretenses . . .

Orgon
Ah! You defy me? You insult him? A stick! A stick! [*To Tartuffe.*] Don't try to stop me. [*To his son.*] Right, leave now, and don't you dare to come back.

Damis
Yes, I'll leave, but . . .

Orgon
Hurry up! Out of here. I'm taking away your inheritance and giving you my curse.

---

6. See the note on this sentence on pages 124–25.

Scene 7

ORGON, TARTUFFE

Orgon
To insult such a holy person!

Tartuffe
Dear Heaven! Pardon him for the pain he has given me! [*To Orgon.*] If you could imagine how dreadful it is to see someone trying to defame me to my dear brother . . .

Orgon
Alas . . .

Tartuffe
Just the thought of this ingratitude is pure torture to me . . . The horror . . . My heart is so heavy that I cannot speak; I feel as if I'm about to die.

Orgon [*He runs, weeping, to the door through which he chased his son.*]
Wretch! I'm sorry that I held back and didn't destroy you on the spot. Dear brother, please calm yourself; don't become angry.

Tartuffe
I beg you, let us stop talking about this. I see what troubles I have brought upon this house; dear brother, I think I must leave.

Orgon
What? Are you joking?

Tartuffe
Everyone hates me, and I see all too well that they doubt my loyalty.

Orgon
What difference does that make? Do you see me paying attention to them?

Tartuffe
They won't stop doing it, and the stories you reject now may one day seem believable.

Orgon
No, dear brother, never.

Tartuffe
Oh, my brother, a woman can very easily dominate her husband.

Orgon
No, no.

Tartuffe
Let me leave quickly so that I can remove all cause for complaint.

Orgon
No, you'll stay: my life depends on it.

Tartuffe
Ah well, then I shall have to mortify myself. But, if you insist . . .

Orgon
Ah!

Tartuffe, Act III, scene 7

Tartuffe
Right, we'll say no more. But I know what must be done. One's reputation is a delicate matter, and to prevent anyone from gossiping or taking umbrage, I shall avoid your wife, and you will not see me . . .

Orgon
No. To spite them, you must visit her frequently. Infuriating people is my greatest joy. I want you to be seen with her at all hours of the day. And that's not all: I'll defy them further by making you my heir, right now, fair and square, and I'll give you all that I have. A true and honest friend, whom I will have for my son-in-law, is dearer to me than son, wife, family. Will you accept what I offer?

Tartuffe
In all things may Heaven's will be done.

Orgon
The poor fellow! Come, we'll write the document and let the others choke on their envy.

Act IV

Scene 1

CLÉANTE, TARTUFFE

Cléante
Yes, everyone is talking about it. Trust me when I tell you that what people are saying doesn't reflect well on you. I'm glad I met you, Monsieur, so that I could tell you exactly what I think. I haven't investigated everything that people are saying; I'll assume it's true and start with what I believe is the worst part. Granted that Damis didn't behave well and that people are accusing you falsely, wouldn't a true Christian forgive him and stifle his instinct for revenge? Is this incident a reason to let a father drive his son away? I must tell you—speaking frankly— that everyone is scandalized by this; if you believe what I've told you, you should make peace between the two of them and not push things to extremes. Let go of your resentment, sacrifice it to God, and reconcile the son and his father.

Tartuffe
Alas! I would love to; I feel no bitterness toward him. I pardon him; I do not accuse him of anything. With all my heart I'd like to help him, but that would not be in the best interests

of Heaven. If he comes back, I will have to leave. After his unbelievable performance, any relations between us would be scandalous. God knows what people would think! They would assume that I was being devious, that, knowing I'm guilty, I'm simply pretending to be charitable so that I could catch him and force him to be silent.

Cléante
No phony excuses, please, Monsieur; they are quite threadbare. Has Heaven made you responsible for its interests? If it wants to punish the guilty, does it need your help? Leave vengeance to God. Instead you should remember His insistence that we forgive the sins of others, and not substitute human legalisms for God's commands. Come on! Can a foolish concern for what people think keep you from the glory of a noble act? No, no: let's do what Heaven commands and not let other worries distract and confuse us.

Tartuffe
I've already told you that my heart forgives him, and that is what Heaven commands. But after today's shocking insults, Heaven does not command that I live with him.

Cléante
Does it command you to obey his father's capricious act and to accept the gift of a fortune that the law forbids you to claim?

Tartuffe
Those who know me will not believe that I act out of self-interest. Worldly goods have no attraction for me; I'm not dazzled by their deceitful appearance. If I have decided to accept the gift his father wishes to give me, it's only, I assure you, because I fear it may fall into unworthy hands, that those who share it will use it for some criminal purpose, and not—as I will—for the glory of the Lord and the welfare of my neighbor.

Tartuffe, Act IV, scene 1

Cléante
Come, come, Monsieur, don't let excessive scruples persuade you that the rightful heir could behave that way. Let him have his inheritance and run the risk himself without your interference. And consider: if he were to misuse it, that would be better for you than being accused of trying to take it from him. I'm surprised that you had no misgivings about permitting this; does religious zeal include the precept that one should defraud the rightful heir? And if Heaven does teach you that there is an invincible obstacle to living with Damis, shouldn't you, as a virtuous man, withdraw honorably rather than allow the family's son to be driven out on account of you? Believe me, Monsieur, that would give your rectitude . . .

Tartuffe
It is, Monsieur, three-thirty. A pious duty requires me to go upstairs; please excuse me now.

Cléante
Ah!

Scene 2

Elmire, Mariane, Cléante, Dorine

Dorine [*To Cléante.*]
Dear Monsieur, please help us with Mariane. She is horribly unhappy; the arrangements that her father made for this evening have pushed her to despair. Here he comes. We're all so upset. Please work with us; somehow or other, we must stop this terrible plan.

Scene 3

ORGON, ELMIRE, MARIANE,
CLÉANTE, DORINE

Orgon
Ah! I'm delighted to see you all together. [*To Mariane.*] I'm carrying a contract that will please you, and you know already what it says.

Mariane [*Kneeling.*]
Please, Father, in the name of Heaven, release me from my misery, from my vows of filial piety, from the obedience that could push me to confess to Heaven that the life you gave me is now a torment. If you must take away my hopes and forbid me to marry the man I love, I beseech you, on my knees — save me from being given to someone I abhor; don't force me to a desperate act by insisting on your power.

Orgon [*He feels himself weakening.*]
Come, be strong, my heart: no human weakness.

Mariane
Your affection for him doesn't hurt me. Let it shine, give him everything you own, and if you need more, give him what is mine as well. I consent willingly; I surrender all that I have to you. But don't give *me* to him; instead let me enter a convent and live under its discipline for the rest of my days.

Tartuffe, Act IV, scene 3

Orgon
Oh yes, women become very religious when their fathers challenge their romantic ideas! Stand up! The more your heart rejects him, the more meritorious it will be to accept him. You want to mortify yourself: you can do so in this marriage. Stop irritating me!

Dorine
But what . . .

Orgon
Quiet, you! You can gossip with your cronies, but I forbid you to say another word here.

Cléante
If you would permit a word of advice . . .

Orgon
Brother, your advice is the best in the world, well thought out, admirable. But excuse me for not taking any of it.

Elmire [*To her husband.*]
I don't know what to say when I see all this; your blindness astonishes me. He must have intoxicated you and warned you well since you spring this on us now.

Orgon
With respect, Madame, I know what I have seen. As for that scoundrel my son, I know how you spoil him. You were afraid to condemn him for playing a trick on this poor fellow; well, you were too calm to be believable. You should have been more upset.

Elmire
Does a foolish declaration of love really threaten a woman's honor? Must we glare and insult people when they say such

things to us? As far as I'm concerned, statements like his make me laugh; I dislike making a fuss about them. I prefer quiet good manners; I don't want to be one of those screeching prudes who defend their honor with claws and teeth and insist on scratching faces. Heaven keep me from such behavior! A virtuous woman doesn't need to act like a spitfire; a cool rejection is quite enough to discourage a lover.

Orgon
Well, I know what happened, and I won't change my mind.

Elmire
I must say, I continue to be amazed by your stubbornness. Would you change your mind if I showed that we are all telling the truth?

Orgon
Showed?

Elmire
Yes.

Orgon
Nonsense.

Elmire
How so? If I could prove it without a doubt?

Orgon
Empty talk.

Elmire
What a man! At least answer me. I am not asking you to trust us. But what if you were in a place where you could see and hear everything, what would you say about your righteous man then?

Tartuffe, Act IV, scene 3

Orgon
In that case, I would say . . . I would say . . . I would say nothing; such things are impossible.

Elmire
You've accused me of telling untruths long enough. I want you, without moving one inch, to be a witness to what I have said.

Orgon
Right. I'll take you at your word. Let's see how clever you are and whether you can keep your promise.

Elmire
Ask him to come here.

Dorine
He's very clever; it may not be easy to trick him.

Elmire
No, it's easy to be fooled by what we want; our vanity is always ready to betray us. [*Speaking to Cléante and Mariane.*] Have him come here, and you go away.

Scene 4

ELMIRE, ORGON

Elmire [*To Orgon.*]
Come here and get underneath this table.

Orgon
What?

Elmire
You have to hide.

Orgon
Why under the table?

Elmire
Oh good Heavens, just do it. I have a plan, and you'll be the judge. Hide, I tell you, and when you're under there, make sure that no one sees or hears you.

Orgon
I must say I'm putting up with a lot; remember, if there are any difficulties, you'll have to get out of them by yourself.

Elmire
I don't think you will have anything to complain about. [*To Orgon, who has hidden under the table.*] I warn you: I'm going to

start in a very strange way; don't let yourself be shocked. No matter what I say, let me say it; I'm doing it to convince you, as I promised. To get that hypocrite to take off his mask, I'll have to act very sweetly, play up to his lecherous advances, let him behave brazenly. I'm doing it only for you, and I'm doing it to trap him—I'll pretend to encourage him until you're convinced, and I'll stop the moment you ask me to. You'll be the one to put an end to his crazy passion as soon as you think he has gone far enough—you'll save me from any more shame once you have seen what you need. You'll protect your interests; you'll be the master, and . . . Here he comes. Don't let him see you.

Scene 5

TARTUFFE, ELMIRE, ORGON

Tartuffe
I was told that you wanted to see me here.

Elmire
Yes, I have something a bit private to tell you. But close that door before I say more, and look everywhere to be sure no one can overhear us. We don't need more incidents like the one that just happened. I've never been so startled in all my life; what Damis did terrified me on your behalf. You saw how I tried to disrupt his scheme and calm him down. I must say that I was so dismayed that I couldn't think of how to contradict him. But happily all ended well, and the situation is much better now. Everyone so respects you that the storm has blown over. My husband cannot possibly take offense: indeed, to put a stop to any malicious gossip, he wants us to be together as much as possible. That's why I'm able to be here alone with you without fear of scandal and to reveal, perhaps a bit too quickly, a heart that's receptive to your passion.

Tartuffe
Such words are difficult to understand, given the way you spoke just a few moments ago.

Tartuffe, Act IV, scene 5

Elmire
Oh, did what I said then trouble you? How little you know of a woman's heart if you didn't understand why my reaction was so lukewarm! Modesty is always fighting with desire. No matter how much love persuades us, we always feel a tiny bit of shame. So we start by pushing our lover away, but anyone can see that our hearts have yielded. We say one thing and mean another; rejecting is really a promise of something else. I'm admitting all this because my modesty has given up the fight. But since I've begun to speak freely—would I have tried to restrain Damis, would I have listened so carefully to your offer of love, would I have behaved as I did if your proposition hadn't pleased me? And when I pushed you to reject that marriage, shouldn't that have hinted at my own interests, my distress that this wedding would force me to share a heart that I wanted for my own?

Tartuffe
It is, dear Madame, a delight to hear such words from someone whom one loves. The honey that trickles through me is one that the mouth has never tasted. My only concern is the joy of pleasing you; my heart is blessed by your confessions. But I hope you will allow that heart to feel a bit uncertain of its happiness. You might simply be trying—honorably—to break off the proposed marriage. Let me be frank: I cannot trust those delicious words you have spoken unless you give me some evidence that you really mean them; your behavior must assure me of your feelings.

Elmire [*She coughs to warn her husband.*]
What? Do you want to move so quickly, to have me reveal all my affection at once? I have tortured myself by making this confession; isn't that enough for you? Will you only be satisfied by my complete surrender?

Tartuffe, Act IV, scene 5

Tartuffe
The less merit one has, the less one dares to hope. Words alone, in these matters, are little reassurance. We may imagine all sorts of good fortune; we must enjoy it before we believe in it. Since I do not believe I deserve your kindness, I cannot believe the happiness I dare to dream of. Indeed, I cannot believe anything, dear Madame, until actions themselves convince me.

Elmire
Lord! Your love is tyrannical; it insists on what it wants so violently! I feel overwhelmed! Come on—can't I prepare properly? Couldn't you give me a moment to breathe? Is it right to push me like this, to demand what you want the moment you want it? You risk jeopardizing your good reputation when you take advantage of it.

Tartuffe
But if you welcome my advances, why refuse more direct proofs?

Elmire
How could I consent without offending Heaven, of which you speak so often?

Tartuffe
If it's only Heaven that stands between us, that's easy for me to deal with; that should certainly not make you hold back.

Elmire
But Heaven's laws are so frightening!

Tartuffe
Let me chase away your foolish fears, Madame; I know how to dismiss such scruples. It's true that Heaven forbids certain pleasures [*A villain speaks these lines.*], but it's possible to make bargains. Depending on what's needed, there are ways to

accommodate our consciences and to justify bad acts by the purity of our intentions. I can be your teacher, Madame; you have only to let me be your guide. Satisfy my desire; never fear, I'll answer for it all and take your sin on my shoulders.—You have a bad cough, Madame.

Elmire
Yes, it's torturing me.

Tartuffe
May I offer you a bit of licorice?

Elmire
It's a stubborn cold; I fear there's no remedy for it.

Tartuffe
That certainly is a shame.

Elmire
Yes, more than I can say.

Tartuffe
In the end, I assure you, it's easy to dismiss your scruples. I promise complete secrecy; only when others make a fuss can there be any harm. Something is scandalous only when it is known; sin that no one knows is no sin.

Elmire [*Having coughed again.*]
Well, I see I must surrender, and let you have your way. I can't expect you to be content with less. I give in. I'm sorry that things have gone so far, that I must yield despite myself. But since you insist on it, since you won't believe what I have said, and require more convincing proof, I'm forced to make you happy. If doing so carries with it some guilt, so much the worse for the one who forces me; surely I am blameless.

Tartuffe, Act IV, scene 5

Tartuffe
Yes indeed, Madame; I am responsible, and the act in itself . . .

Elmire
Please open that door, and look to be sure that my husband isn't in the hall.

Tartuffe
What need to be so careful? He is, between us, a man you can lead by the nose; he's proud of our relationship, and I've persuaded him to see everything and to believe nothing.

Elmire
Never mind that; please take a good look.

Scene 6

ORGON, ELMIRE

Orgon [*Climbing out from under the table.*]
What an abominable man! I can't believe it! I'm overwhelmed!

Elmire
What? You're coming out so soon? Don't be silly. Go back under; it's not yet time to come out. Just wait to the end to be sure of what you see; don't trust your suspicions.

Orgon
No. Nothing more wicked ever came out of Hell.

Elmire
Goodness, don't be too quick to believe. Go slowly; let yourself be thoroughly convinced; wait to be sure you haven't misunderstood. [*She hides her husband behind her.*]

Scene 7

TARTUFFE, ELMIRE, ORGON

Tartuffe
Everything is as I had hoped: I looked everywhere, no one is there, and my delighted soul . . .

Orgon [*Stopping him.*]
Slowly now! Your desire pushes you much too fast; don't become so excited so quickly. Oh, oh, you virtuous man, you want to bless me! How quickly your soul yields to temptation! You'll marry my daughter and seduce my wife! I always wondered what the truth was; I always suspected that you'd change your tune. But I've seen quite enough: I'm satisfied; I don't need to see any more.

Elmire
This is not the way I wanted things to happen, but I was driven to behave this way.

Tartuffe
What? Do you think? . . .

Orgon
That's enough, not another word. Get out of here immediately.

Tartuffe
My plan . . .

Orgon
Your comments are worthless here; leave at once.

Tartuffe
You're the one who has to leave, you, who pretend to be the master. The house belongs to me. I'll make that known, and I'll prove that you have no recourse, no way to challenge me with these cowardly tricks. You can't injure me. I have the power to resist; to face down your claims; to avenge Heaven, which you have attacked; to make you sorry you tried to throw me out.

Scene 8

ELMIRE, ORGON

Elmire
What is he saying? What does he mean?

Orgon
I don't know; this is no laughing matter.

Elmire
What?

Orgon
I see how wrong I was; I should never have made that gift.

Elmire
Gift?

Orgon
Yes, it's signed and sealed, and there's something else that worries me.

Elmire
What's that?

Orgon
I'll tell you in a moment. Right now I've got to be sure that my little box is upstairs.

Act V

Scene 1

ORGON, CLÉANTE

Cléante
Where are you going?

Orgon
Damn! I don't know!

Cléante
I think you and I should talk about the best thing to do in the circumstances.

Orgon
That little box is on my mind; I'm more worried about it than about anything else.

Cléante
What's in that mysterious box?

Tartuffe, Act V, scene 1

Orgon
Argas, that friend for whom I feel so sorry, secretly gave it to me as he was escaping; he said it contained papers on which his life and his possessions depend.

Cléante
Then why did you let someone else have it?

Orgon
It was on my conscience. I went to that traitor to confide in him; he persuaded me that I should let him guard the box so that if Argas were investigated, I'd be able to deny having done him a favor: that way, telling a lie wouldn't be on my conscience.

Cléante
As I understand it, you're in trouble. Let me speak candidly: you don't seem to have taken your responsibility for the box and the secret seriously enough. Promises like that have significant consequences. You'll have to approach Tartuffe more tactfully, so that his hold on you doesn't become stronger.

Orgon
Damn! To hide deceit and wickedness under such a fine appearance of piety! And I welcomed him as a poor beggar who had nothing . . . That's it! I'm finished with all these virtuous souls; I'll avoid them like the plague and become worse than any devil.

Cléante
Come on! You've blustered enough! You always exaggerate; you lack judgment; you throw yourself from one extreme to the other. You see that you were wrong, that phony piety took advantage of you: but why correct one mistake by rushing into another that's even worse? Just because you've known one scoundrel, do you think that everyone else is just as bad?

Tartuffe, Act V, scene 1

Here's a knave who deceived you brazenly by pretending to be a pious ascetic; do you think everyone is like him, that there are no truly religious people? Let freethinkers have foolish ideas like those; you should distinguish between mere appearances and true virtue. Avoid taking impostors too seriously, but don't insult real commitment. If you insist on leaning too far to one side or the other, try to err on the side of generosity.

Scene 2

DAMIS, ORGON, CLÉANTE

Damis
Father, is it true that this rogue is threatening you? That he's forgotten all the benefits he has received? Is that arrogant coward—who deserves to be punished—using your gifts against you?

Orgon
Yes, Son, it's true. No one has ever suffered as I do.

Damis
I'll cut off his ears; we can't ignore his insolence. I must free you of him at once; I must kill him.

Cléante
There speaks a brave little lad; come on, calm down. We live under the rule of law; we can't take violence into our own hands.

Scene 3

MME. PERNELLE, MARIANE, ELMIRE,
DORINE, DAMIS, ORGON, CLÉANTE

Mme. Pernelle
What's all this? I've been hearing terribly strange stories.

Orgon
Unheard-of things have happened, which I've seen with my own eyes. Just look at what my good deeds have cost me. I eagerly welcomed a miserable man, housed him, considered him my brother, loaded him with gifts, promised him my daughter and all my possessions. And meanwhile this traitor, this wretch, tried to seduce my wife; and as if that hadn't been enough, he's taking advantage of my benevolence to threaten me. He wants to ruin me by using the gifts I foolishly gave him; he wants to drive me from my house and reduce me to the condition in which I found him.

Dorine
The poor fellow.

Mme. Pernelle
My son, I cannot possibly believe that he would have done such a vile deed.

Orgon
Pardon?

Mme. Pernelle
Worthy folks are always envied.

Orgon
What in the world do you mean by that remark, Mother?

Mme. Pernelle
That people carry on in strange ways here, and everyone knows how much he is hated.

Orgon
What does hate have to do with what you have heard?

Mme. Pernelle
When you were a little boy I told you this a hundred times: virtue is always a target — envious people may die; envy doesn't.

Orgon
But what does that lesson have to do with what is happening today?

Mme. Pernelle
People have been saying ridiculous things about him.

Orgon
I tell you I saw it all with my own eyes.

Mme. Pernelle
Spiteful gossipers tell dreadful stories.

Orgon
You're pushing me to extremes, Mother. I tell you I saw this brazen behavior with my own eyes.

Mme. Pernelle
Nothing in this world can deflect the venom of malice.

Orgon
What you are saying makes no sense at all. I tell you I saw what I saw, myself, with my own eyes. Do I have to box your ears to make you listen?

Mme. Pernelle
My Lord! You know how often appearances can be deceptive; you mustn't always believe what you see.

Orgon
I can't stand this.

Mme. Pernelle
Everyone is a victim of false suspicion, and sometimes even good deeds are misinterpreted.

Orgon
Am I to believe that he tried to seduce my wife simply out of Christian charity?

Mme. Pernelle
If you are going to accuse someone, you have to have a good reason and be absolutely sure of what you know.

Orgon
Damn it all! Be absolutely sure? So I was supposed to wait until I saw him . . . I was about to say something indecent.

Mme. Pernelle
It's true that he can be overzealous, but I cannot possibly bring myself to believe that he tried to do the things he is said to have done.

Orgon
Look here! If you weren't my mother, I don't know what I'd do.

Dorine
Turn about is fair play, Monsieur: you didn't want to believe, and no one believes you.

Cléante
We're wasting time with this foolish talk; we should be using it to stop this wretch who's threatening us all.

Damis
How far do you think he'll dare to go?

Elmire
This lawsuit seems ridiculous. Who could take it seriously? Isn't his ingratitude all too obvious?

Cléante
Don't be too sure; he has the means to prove you wrong. Even a flimsy scheme can trap people when a clique supports it. I'll say it again: with the resources he has, he shouldn't be confronted directly.

Orgon
True enough, but what to do? I'm infuriated when I think about this traitor's arrogance.

Cléante
I really wish that there could be some way to reconcile the two of you.

Elmire
If I'd known the weapons he held, I would never have provoked him, and my . . .

Orgon
What does that man want? Go and find out right away! I'm in no condition to see anyone.

Scene 4

M. Loyal, Mme. Pernelle,
Orgon, Damis, Mariane,
Dorine, Elmire, Cléante

M. Loyal
Good morning, my dear sister; please allow me to speak to Monsieur.

Dorine
He has company with him; I doubt that he would be able to see someone.

M. Loyal
I do not wish to intrude. I believe that my mission, rather than causing him any discomfort, will please him.

Dorine
Your name?

M. Loyal
Just tell him that I have come on behalf of Monsieur Tartuffe, on a matter that will, he says, be gratifying.

Dorine
There's a soft-spoken man who comes, he says, from Monsieur Tartuffe on a matter that will, he says, be gratifying.

Cléante
We'll have to see this man and find out what he wants.

Orgon
Maybe he has come to settle our differences. How should I treat him?

Cléante
Don't let him see that you're angry, and if he speaks about coming to some arrangement, you must listen to him.

M. Loyal
Greetings, Monsieur. May Heaven vanquish those who wish to harm you; my wish is that all may go well for you.

Orgon
This affable introduction makes me feel better; perhaps there can be some accommodation.

M. Loyal
Your family has always been dear to me, and I was a servant of your honorable father.

Orgon
Monsieur, I am ashamed that I do not recognize you and ask you to forgive me for not knowing your name.

M. Loyal
My name is Loyal; I am from Normandy, a beadle, who has for forty years honorably filled that position, thanks be to God. With your permission, Monsieur, I have come with a court order to dispossess . . .

Orgon
What! You have come . . .

Tartuffe, Act V, scene 4

M. Loyal
Monsieur, calm yourself; it's only an order to leave the premises, you and your family, put your furniture out, make room for someone else without delay, as the situation requires . . .

Orgon
Me? Leave the premises?

M. Loyal
Yes, Monsieur, if you please. As everyone knows, the house now belongs entirely to our good Monsieur Tartuffe. He's the owner of all your holdings, by virtue of a contract that I have here. It's properly executed; it cannot be challenged.

Damis
What unbelievable insolence! I've never seen anything like it.

M. Loyal
Monsieur, I have no business with you; I address myself to this gentleman. He is reasonable and calm, and since he knows the way a respectable man should behave, I am sure he will not oppose the law.

Orgon
But . . .

M. Loyal
Monsieur, I know that you would not obstruct justice for anything in the world and that, being an honorable person, you will permit me to carry out the orders I have been given.

Damis
Get yourself and your staff of office out of here.

M. Loyal
Monsieur, please tell your son to keep quiet or leave. I should hate to have to make note of all this and add it to my testimony.

Tartuffe, Act V, scene 4

Dorine
This Monsieur Loyal seems to be a pretty disloyal fellow to me!

M. Loyal
I am always perfectly civil to the well-to-do; I was only willing to do this because I wanted to please you and save you from someone who might have less affection for you and would treat you less gently.

Orgon
And what could be worse than telling honest folks that they must leave their home?

M. Loyal
We're giving you time — I won't require you to comply until tomorrow. All I'll do is spend the night here with ten of my men — no fuss, no scenes. Just for the sake of formalities, please give me your keys. I won't disturb you or allow anything inappropriate to happen. But tomorrow you must be quick to empty everything out, right to the last spoon. My people will assist you — I've brought strong men to help you haul everything out of the house. No one could be more generous, in my opinion, and since I'm treating you so kindly, I hope you'll respond as you should and not make any difficulties for me.

Orgon
I'd gladly give a hundred pieces of gold — if I had any — for the pleasure of punching this fellow in the snout.

Cléante
Let it be; don't make matters worse.

Damis
I'm itching to attack this insolent fellow.

Dorine
Since you're so strong and handsome, Monsieur Loyal, I doubt that a few good thwacks with a stick would do you much harm.

M. Loyal
It's quite easy to punish such disrespectful talk, Miss, and laws apply to women as well as to men.

Cléante
Enough of all this, Monsieur; please give me the summons, and leave us alone.

M. Loyal
Until tomorrow. May Heaven bless you all!

Orgon
May it curse you and the one who sent you!

Scene 5

Orgon, Cléante, Mariane, Elmire,
Mme. Pernelle, Dorine, Damis

Orgon
Well, Mother, now do you see that I was right? What just happened confirms what I told you. Now will you acknowledge his treachery?

Mme. Pernelle
I'm speechless; I can't believe my ears!

Dorine
Don't complain or blame him. His pious wishes have come true. He cares for the welfare of others; he knows that worldly wealth often corrupts, and out of pure charity he has taken it from you to save you.

Orgon
Once again: be quiet!

Cléante
Let's see whether we can get some useful advice.

Elmire
Go—tell everyone about the way this traitor lied to us. Behavior like that must surely void any contract. Once people know how he betrayed us, no one will let him succeed.

Scene 6

Valère, Orgon, Cléante,
Elmire, Mariane,
Mme. Pernelle,
Damis, Dorine

Valère
Monsieur, I'm deeply sorry to disturb you now, but in the present circumstances I feel I must. A very close friend who knows my concern for you has told me a state secret; something has happened that means you'll have to flee. That villain who took such advantage of you has denounced you to the King, accusing you of treason, and has given him that box that you had hidden. I don't know what crime you are accused of, but a summons against you has been sworn and Tartuffe himself is ordered to come with the officer who is to arrest you.

Cléante
So this is his weapon! That's how he thinks he can claim all your possessions!

Orgon
Animals: that's what men are!

Valère
Any delay may be fatal. My carriage is waiting at the door to take you away, and here are a thousand pieces of gold. Lose

no time. This is an explosive situation; the only way to defend yourself is to run from it. I promise to lead you to a safe place, and I'll go with you all the way.

Orgon
Oh Lord! How grateful I am for your kindness! I'll have to thank you properly at another time; I hope Heaven will allow me to recognize your generosity properly. Good-bye, take care of yourselves . . .

Cléante
Go quickly, Brother; we'll think about what to do.

Last Scene

THE OFFICER, TARTUFFE,
VALÈRE, ORGON, ELMIRE,
MARIANE, MME. PERNELLE,
DORINE, CLÉANTE, DAMIS

Tartuffe
Just a moment, Monsieur, just a moment, not so fast. You won't need to go far to find a place to stay. You are a prisoner, by order of the King.

Orgon
So, you snake in the grass; you kept this blow for last. Is this the way you'll destroy me? Is your treachery complete? Is this the final touch?

Tartuffe
Your insults cannot annoy me; Heaven has taught me to endure all for its sake.

Cléante
Admirable restraint!

Damis
Listen to him shamelessly taking the name of Heaven in vain!

Tartuffe
All that ranting fails to disturb me; I simply want to do my duty.

Tartuffe, Act V, last scene

Mariane
You can surely be proud of what you are doing—this act is a credit to you.

Tartuffe
Any act on behalf of the person who sent me here can only be honorable.

Orgon
But have you forgotten that my generosity pulled you out of your misery, you ungrateful wretch?

Tartuffe
Yes, I know what help it might have given me, but the wishes of the King are my first obligation. The justifiable urgency of that sacred duty stifles any gratitude in my heart, and to that duty I would sacrifice even more powerful demands: friends, wife, family, even myself.

Elmire
Fraud!

Dorine
How neatly he dresses up his treachery in pious words.

Cléante
But if this religious zeal that you claim and boast about is so perfect, how is it that Orgon found you making love to his wife? Why did you wait to denounce him until his own honor forced him to chase you out? I'll say nothing at this point about the fact that he gave you all his wealth, but why are you still willing to accept it when you claim he is a traitor?

Tartuffe [*To the officer of the court who has come with him.*]
Monsieur, stop all this nonsense, please, and get on with the orders you have been given.

Tartuffe, Act V, last scene

The Officer
Yes, we have waited too long; you've reminded me to do my duty. My orders, which I will execute, require you to follow me immediately to the prison that has been assigned to you.

Tartuffe
Who? I, Monsieur?

The Officer
Yes, you.

Tartuffe
Why to prison?

The Officer
I am not obliged to give you an explanation. Monsieur [*To Orgon.*], please calm yourself. We live under a king who is the enemy of fraud, a king who is guided by moderation and intelligence, who knows all his subjects, who is never deceived by impostors. Mere acquaintance does not influence him; he knows what the truth is and understands what is happening; he sees to it that honorable men are properly recognized. He loves virtue, but he recognizes the reality of wickedness; a rogue like this might set traps but could never deceive him. The King knows this man's heart; when Tartuffe came to accuse you, he simply revealed his own treachery. Someone else had reported this charlatan's long train of abuses, his cowardly ingratitude and disloyalty. The King let things go this far simply to see how far they would go and to demonstrate conclusively how firmly he could act. Here and now he takes all the documents that this traitor claims are his and nullifies the contract that puts your wealth in his hands. Moreover, in recognition of the zeal you exercised on your monarch's behalf in the past, he pardons you for accepting the secret information that your friend gave you. The King rewards good deeds,

Tartuffe, Act V, last scene

sometimes when it's least expected; he prefers to remember the good than to focus on error.[7]

Dorine
May Heaven be praised!

Mme. Pernelle
I can breathe again.

Elmire
What a wonderful outcome!

Mariane
Who could have dared to expect it?

Orgon [*To Tartuffe.*]
There you are, you traitor . . .

Cléante
Dear brother—stop. Don't stoop to indignity. Leave that miserable person to his misfortune; don't add to his remorse. Pray that he'll turn toward virtue, that he'll change his way of life and reject his vices, and that our great monarch will moderate his strict justice. Go to the King; acknowledge his magnanimity, and thank him for his kindness toward you.

Orgon
Yes, well said; let's go gratefully to the King to praise his generosity. And once we have begun to pay our debt to him, let's think of someone else's happiness and reward Valère's devotion and sincerity by celebrating his marriage to Mariane.

The End

---

7. See the note on this speech on pages 125–27.

Notes to *Tartuffe*

Note on the names of characters in *Tartuffe*

We meet the characters before the curtain goes up, each (save three) defined by his or her relationship with the other characters. Mme. Pernelle, mother of Orgon; Orgon, husband of Elmire; Elmire, wife of Orgon; Damis, son of Orgon; Mariane, daughter of Orgon and beloved of Valère; Valère, beloved of Mariane; Cléante, brother of Elmire; Tartuffe, a religious hypocrite; Dorine, companion and maid to Mariane; M. Loyal, a beadle; an officer; Flipote, servant of Mme. Pernelle. A perfectly ordinary list—except for the names. It's true that the consonants and vowels in Flipote and Pernelle invite us to think these names are meant to be comical; Mariane is quite conventional, and Valère sounds enough like *valiant* in French to be an appropriate name for a young lover. But what about Orgon, Elmire, Damis, Cléante, and Tartuffe? It's highly unlikely that these were names given at a baptismal font in the Paris of Louis XIV.

Stepping back from *Tartuffe* and looking at *The Misanthrope*, *The School for Wives*, *The Doctor Despite Himself*, and *The Miser*, we see the same pattern of names: some recognizably French, others clearly from some other idiom. To the audience in the theater of 1669, the source was obvious: these non-French names are Greek or pseudo-Greek, taken directly from the classics or copied from the novels and poems of the *Précieux* and the *Précieuses*, the highly educated nobles and gentlefolk of both sexes who considered themselves arbiters of society, manners, education, and language.

Tartuffe, Notes: Names of Characters

England, Spain, and Italy had had equivalents—the Euphuists in England, the Gongorists in Spain, the Della Cruscans in Florence—but these had not had the influence of the *Précieuses* in France. Parisian society was captivated by the elegance and refinement of the learned ladies whose letters and novels, derived from Greek histories and drama (some of which, like *Artamène, ou Le Grand Cyrus* by Mme. de Scudéry, extended to several volumes), were impatiently bought, diligently read, and enthusiastically imitated. So the playgoers in the theater of the Palais Royal or at Versailles recognized the names in Molière's comedies as soon as they heard them.

The name they did not recognize was Tartuffe. Some scholars believe that the name came from the Italian *tartufo,* or truffle: bulgy and subterranean, a fungus attached to the roots of noble trees like oaks and beeches. Others think Molière simply invented it. In either case, it was an announcement to the audience that this character emerged from a context different from that of the elegant and learned *Précieux.*

Characters in twentieth- and twenty-first-century drama have the same names as we in the audience have. In some cases, dramatists have deliberately started with a real person—*Einstein on the Beach, Nixon in China, The Madness of King George III*—and have invented or extrapolated to create new insights into the conventional understanding of these protagonists. In other plays, less obviously tied to historic figures, the names are those we hear every day. The hero of *Death of a Salesman* is Willy; James, Edmund, and Mary are the principal characters in *A Long Day's Journey into Night;* Shaw's characters include Barbara, Charles, Andrew, Eliza, Freddy, Henry, and Alfred.

Then what was Molière doing when he chose names that reminded his audience of the Greek and Roman classics and of the elaborations of the *Précieux?* The performance history of *Tartuffe* answers the question. First performed in 1664—and immediately banned, revised, performed, and banned again in 1667—it was finally presented in February 1669, and only then was it allowed to continue. With Molière himself playing Orgon, it enjoyed the longest run and the largest box-office receipts of any of Molière's plays.

Religious hypocrisy was an inflammatory topic at that time. It was one thing to present a comedy that criticized the follies or even the vices of the time; it was another to appear to censure the behavior of prelates and their noble supporters who were highly placed political figures. The names allowed Molière to claim that he was writing a general comedy, to put some distance between the characters on the stage and those who might have been their models.

Censorship in the Western world today poses no threat to comedians; writers can afford to name names and point fingers on television, on radio, in the theater, and in the movies. Would a comedy like *Tartuffe* be written today? In what circumstances might playwrights in Paris, London, and New York choose names for their characters that would disguise or dilute the criticism they were making of contemporary figures or morals? By being explicit, what has been lost or gained?

Act I, scene 2: Dorine: "She's nothing compared to her son [Orgon]. . . . In the recent 'troubles' he was known as a level-headed man who backed his king courageously."

"Troubles" is a tactful reference to almost a decade of civil war in France, a period of intrigue and shifting political and familial loyalties. The first manifestation of these troubles was called the Fronde (Uprising) of the Parlement (1648–1649). Anne of Austria, mother as well as regent for her son Louis XIV, and her chief minister, Cardinal Mazarin, decreed that the crown would raise revenue by stopping the pay of all magistrates of the high court for four years. In return, the Parlement presented a document severely limiting the power of the crown. Members of the Parlement, led by the Prince of Condé and Armand de Conti (one of Molière's patrons), were arrested; riots ensued; and royal troops besieged Paris until an agreement was reached with the Parlement in 1649.

But the nobles resented the power of Anne of Austria and Cardinal Mazarin and in 1650 began a second Fronde. The Prince of Condé, in alliance with the king of Spain, again provoked battles elsewhere in France and riots in Paris that drove Anne of Austria, the young Louis XIV, and Cardinal Mazarin out of the city for almost two years. Long negotiations re-established royal power, although real domestic peace was not finally confirmed until 1658.

Molière's major plays were written after 1653, when Paris was once again free to enjoy the theater, the court could indulge in elaborate balls and spectacles, the literary ladies and their salons could meet for untroubled conversation, and the loyal bourgeoisie, from whose ranks the King increasingly drew his most important ministers, could begin to profit from their financial security and social status. Such was Orgon's situation in the world until Tartuffe came into his life and his household.

Act III, scene 2: Tartuffe: "Laurent, put away my hair shirt and my lash."

When at last Tartuffe appears, this is how he introduces himself. Thus far the audience has seen him only indirectly: Dorine described a glutton who boasts of his social standing; Orgon described a man so tenderhearted that he grieves over a squeezed louse; Mme. Pernelle said that Heaven sent him to Orgon's house; Mariane said she would rather die than marry him; Damis called him an oaf. Where do the hair shirt and the lash fit into this kaleidoscopic portrait?

Tartuffe, Notes: Act III, scene 2

Although some monks and priests in seventeenth-century Paris may have used hair shirts and lashes, Tartuffe—a layman, plump, with rosy lips—is highly unlikely to have used such stringent methods of self-discipline. Molière assumes that his audience will know this is a pose; he also assumes that his audience knew where to place Tartuffe in the landscape of religious controversies that engaged the court, the clergy, and the laymen of his day.

Louis XIV ruled by "divine right"; his political advisors were cardinals and priests as well as laymen. All capitals are places for cabals (Molière uses this term freely in his plays), power and pressure groups that included nobles and merchants, priests and laity, the discreetly virtuous as well as the doctrinaire reformers. A number of these zealots belonged to the Confraternity of the Holy Sacrament, a semisecret organization whose members included priests and dukes, some of whom were closely allied with the royal family. Its mission was to care for the poor and to correct the immorality and religious laxity of the times. Lay members occasionally took it upon themselves to join households and become confessors and directors of conscience; some may also have served as conduits of information between the court, the clergy, the nobility, and the prosperous families with which these laymen were connected. Tartuffe, adopted by Orgon's family, might have hoped to be taken for a member of this prestigious confraternity.

Religion and the secular world were tightly entwined in the reign of Louis XIV. Cardinals Richelieu and Mazarin had been prime ministers for Louis XIII, and Mazarin continued in that role for Louis XIV. Bossuet, one of the most rigorous and persuasive of preachers, had succeeded in detaching the King's mistress from him, and although Louis reinstated her officially in his household, the jostling between the worldly and the rigorous factions of the church and its supporters did not entirely subside. When *Tartuffe* was finally performed in 1669, religious cabals and intrigues were still potent, and characters like Tartuffe were quick to take advantage of the moral uneasiness of the times.

Tartuffe, then, was an all-too-recognizable figure. Molière was painting with a very broad brush: Tartuffe—glutton and prude, lecher and ostentatious puritan—had no single model in the court or the city. He was the sum of all religious hypocrites; the hair shirt and the lash (never again mentioned) are disguises that reveal rather than hide his character.

Act III, scene 6: Orgon: "You'll see that you must obey me, that I'm the master here."

Mariane is told she must abandon her beloved; Dorine is told she must be quiet; Elmire is told that sin is no disgrace. Orgon and Tartuffe believe that men are the masters; we do not. The women in *Tartuffe*, as in many of Molière's plays, are in fact those who move the plot along, who straighten out the complications, who avert the bad results of foolish decisions.

In some circles of the French bourgeoisie and the nobility, the seventeenth century was an era of powerful women. Anne of Austria, the wife and then the widow of Louis XIII, was the regent of France in name and in fact until her death; her political and religious expectations and decisions stirred up controversies and smoothed them over. Louis XIV's wife and his mistresses continued this pattern of influence. The *Précieuses*—the learned ladies who set the tone for language and amorous behavior— attracted the attention of courtiers and authors, painters and musicians, grammarians and leaders of armies. For Molière, these learned ladies were sometimes the object of comedy, even mockery, but in the more serious plays—*Tartuffe, The Misanthrope, The Miser, The School for Wives*—the women are as significant as the men, and often even more powerful.

Their power is the power of common sense. In Act III, scenes 4 and 5, Elmire says, "All [Tartuffe] has to do is to behave better and try to be worthy of my generosity. . . . I'm not inclined to make trouble. Real women laugh at such foolishness; they don't bother to tell their husbands about it. . . . Honor doesn't depend on reporting silliness like this; all that's necessary is to defend oneself against it: at least that's my opinion." Damis, Elmire's hot-tempered stepson, is ready to attack Tartuffe; Orgon is ready to beat Damis with a stick; Valère, willfully misunderstanding Mariane, rejects her. Elmire and Dorine will have none of this; theirs are the voices of moderation.

There were, of course, extravagant women in as well as outside of Molière's plays. Their contemporaries recognized the ridiculous and pretentious ladies of *Les Précieuses Ridicules* and *Les Femmes Savantes* and their equivalents who slavishly and indiscriminately copied the modes of speech and behavior of authors and leaders of society like Mme. de Scudéry, Mme. de Sévigné, and Mme. de Lafayette. Opinionated and stubborn old women, saucy and meddling maids who irritate their masters and mistresses—stock figures in comedy and daily gossip everywhere—were equally well known. But Molière's job was to hold up a mirror to all of society. It's important to see, reflected in that mirror, the temperate, wise, quiet, and effective women: they too were a recognized and important part of his world.

Act V, Last Scene: The Officer: "The King rewards good deeds."

The court and the theater were, at times, one and the same during the reign of Louis XIV. When the king greeted ambassadors from foreign countries, the receptions were as thoroughly stage-managed and costumed as any theatrical performance. Kings were expected to dazzle their subjects as well as to govern them; like the signing of peace treaties, royal marriages and

Tartuffe, Notes: Act V, last scene

births were occasions to transform Versailles, the Louvre, and the Palais Royal into spaces for elaborate performances of comedies, tragedies, ballets, and farces, accompanied by music and enhanced by theatrical machinery.

Molière was not an invisible playwright. The King knew him, had commissioned many of Molière's plays, and had, shortly before the first performance of *Tartuffe,* served as godfather to Molière's first son. More, the King had performed in some of Molière's plays, had made suggestions for an addition to one of them, and had paid for the costumes, the musicians, and the theatrical machinery necessary for plots that included disguises, betrayals, and revelations at the last minute. He would have recognized the King's officer, appearing like a deus ex machina to resolve the drama, as a device that fit easily into a familiar pattern of comedy and stagecraft.

Nonetheless, this ending seems abrupt, unexpected, even unsatisfactory. At the beginning of the eighteenth century, the play was translated into English by a certain M. Medbourne, who explained that he had "render'd [it] into English, with much addition and advantage." Those additions and advantages were changes that allowed the other characters—Dorine and Laurent, Cléante and Elmire, Valère and Mariane—to construct a counterplot in which to trap Tartuffe without recourse to the sudden appearance of the King's emissary.

Although Medbourne thought that Molière's ending required "addition and advantage," it is possible that Molière's audiences disagreed because they recognized a second drama being enacted at the end of this comedy. In the almost five years since Molière had first presented *Tartuffe,* it had been repeatedly banned by the archbishop of Paris despite the tacit and explicit approval of Louis XIV himself, who saw the first performance and found it entertaining. Molière had written a preface to the play and two appeals to the King, explaining that he meant no disrespect to the Church and intended only to criticize those who disgraced it by behaving like hypocrites. But it required the personal intervention of the King before the play could open in February 1669. The unexpected appearance of the King's officer, the long speech in praise of the King—"a king who is the enemy of fraud, a king who is guided by moderation and intelligence, who knows all his subjects, who is never deceived by impostors," who recognized "the zeal [Orgon] exercised on [his] monarch's behalf"—this abrupt reversal that saves Orgon served also as Molière's tribute to the King, his friend, who had at last allowed his play to be seen.

First Appeal

Presented to the King
Concerning the comedy of *Tartuffe*

Sire:
Since the task of comedy is to reform men while amusing them, I thought that, given the work I do, I could do nothing better than to attack by caricature the vices of my age; and since hypocrisy is, without doubt, one of the most common, the most harmful, and the most dangerous of these, I thought, Sire, that I would render no small service to all the honorable men of your kingdom if I were to make a comedy that would discredit the hypocrites and present all the artificial gestures that these worthy folk display, all the hidden deceptions of these counterfeit saints who want to entrap men by their spurious zeal and compromising morals.

I wrote this comedy, Sire, as carefully as I could and with all the circumspection that the delicate nature of the topic required; and to preserve the honor and respect owed to those who are truly devout, I was at pains to distinguish them from the character that I was presenting. I included nothing that might appear equivocal; I omitted anything that could confuse good with ill and used, in this portrait, only the colors and the essential characteristics that reveal the true and accomplished hypocrite.

Nonetheless, my precautions were useless. People have, Sire, taken advantage of your sensitivity to religious affairs and have attacked you in the only place where you might be vulnerable — that is, your respect for sacred matters. The tartuffes, disguised, were clever enough to find favor with Your Majesty, and those who were its originals suppressed the copy, however innocent it may have been and however recognizable some may have found it.

As strong a blow as this suppression of my work might have been, my distress was nonetheless softened by the way in which Your Majesty explained himself; and truly, Sire, this removed all cause for complaint, since Your Majesty had the goodness to state that he found no cause for complaint in the comedy that I had been forbidden to present to the public.

But, despite this gracious statement by the world's greatest and most enlightened king, despite the approval of the Pope's emissary and the greater number of our prelates who all, in the private readings that I presented to them, agreed with Your Majesty's sentiments, despite all this, I say, we have seen a book written by the curé of . . .[1] that noisily challenges these honorable opinions. Despite what Your Majesty may have said, despite the opinions of the Pope's emissary and the prelates, my comedy, said he without having seen it, is as diabolic as is my brain; I am a demon clothed in flesh and dressed like a man, licentious, an apostate worthy of extraordinary punishment. Burning my book in public is not sufficient expiation—that would let me off too easily. The charitable zeal of this gallant gentleman does not stop there: he wishes to deny me God's mercy; he has absolutely decided that I should be damned.

This book, Sire, was presented to Your Majesty, and Your Majesty can without doubt understand how distressing it is for me to see myself exposed daily to these insults, the damage that such calumny does to me if indeed it must be tolerated, the need I have to clear myself of these fabrications and to show to the public that my comedy is nothing but what one might wish it to be. I will not describe, Sire, what I might need to restore my reputation and to demonstrate to all the innocence of my work; enlightened kings like yourself need no instruction or requests; they see, as God sees, what is necessary, and they know better

---

1. This is a reference to Pierre Roullé, the curé of Saint-Barthélemy.

Tartuffe, First Appeal

than we do what we should receive. It is enough to put my interests in YOUR MAJESTY'S hands, and I await, with much respect, anything that YOUR MAJESTY should please to command.

Second Appeal

Presented to the King in his camp outside the city of Lille in Flanders, by DE LA THORILLIÈRE and DE LA GRANGE, HIS MAJESTY'S comedians, and colleagues of M. MOLIÈRE, concerning the ban, dated 6 August 1667, that forbade the presentation of *Tartuffe* until HIS MAJESTY should give a new order.

SIRE:
It is a very daring thing for me to importune a great monarch at the time of his glorious conquests; but, given my situation, where, SIRE, could I find protection other than where I have come to seek it? And whom might I enlist to counter the forces that overcome me, if not the source of power and authority, the just dispenser of orders, the sovereign judge and the master of all things?

My comedy, SIRE, cannot enjoy the benefits of YOUR MAJESTY'S kindness. In vain did I produce it under the title of *The Impostor* and disguise the character as a man of the world. In vain did I give him a little hat, a great wig, a big collar, a sword, and lace all over his jacket; soften his behavior; and carefully omit anything that I thought would give the shadow of an excuse to the well-known originals of the portrait I wished to paint: all that was of no avail. The cabal armed itself simply because of what it suspected of the play. They found a way to take by surprise those who, in other respects, boast that they cannot be thus taken. No sooner had my comedy been presented than it was struck by a blow from a force that commands respect; and at that moment all that I could do to save myself from the violence

Tartuffe, Second Appeal

of this tempest was to say that YOUR MAJESTY had had the kindness to allow the performance and that I had not thought it necessary to seek permission from others, since it was only YOUR MAJESTY who might have forbidden it.

I do not doubt, SIRE, that those whom I depict in my comedy have pressed YOUR MAJESTY quite hard and have once again drawn into their party many worthy people who are the more easily deceived because they judge others to be like themselves. Those folks have the skill to dress all their schemes in fine colors. No matter what they may seem to be, it is not God's interests that move them; they have shown this clearly enough by allowing certain comedies to be produced so often without saying a word against them. Those comedies attack piety or religion, which concerns them very little—but this one attacks them and shows them on the stage; that is what they cannot bear. They cannot forgive me for revealing their pretenses to all the world, and certainly none of them will fail to tell YOUR MAJESTY that my comedy has scandalized everyone. But the truth, SIRE, is that all of Paris has been scandalized only by the prohibition, that the truly scrupulous have found the play useful, and that many are surprised that persons so known for probity should have deferred to others who ought to disgust everyone and who are so opposed to the true piety that they themselves profess.

I await with respect YOUR MAJESTY'S decision on this matter, but it is certain, SIRE, that I must no longer think of writing comedies if the tartuffes win the day, that they will feel justified in persecuting me more than ever and will find more to say about the most innocent things that I might write.

Deign in your kindness, SIRE, to protect me from their venomous rage, and may I, when you have returned from your glorious campaign, be capable of giving you some relief from the weariness of your conquests and of entertaining the monarch who makes all Europe tremble.

Third Appeal

Presented to the King
5 February 1669

Sire:

A highly respected physician, one of whose patients I have the honor to be, promises and undertakes, in the presence of a notary, to keep me alive another thirty years if I can persuade Your Majesty to grant him a request. I told him that I do not ask such a promise of him and that I would be satisfied if he would simply have the kindness not to kill me. His request is to be granted a canonical position in the royal chapel at Vincennes, made vacant by the death of . . .

Dare I ask this favor of Your Majesty on the very day of the resurrection of *Tartuffe*, resurrected by your kindness? Thanks to that kindness I have been reconciled with the faithful and, by this one, I will be with the physicians. Perhaps this shows me too much kindness at one time, but perhaps it is not beyond the power of Your Majesty, and I await, with respectful hope, a response to my appeal.

The Misanthrope

Translator's Note: *The Misanthrope*

"Poetry in translation is like a boiled strawberry," the composer Carl Ruggles (1876–1971) is reported to have said, a warning that haunts any translator. Some words are so embedded in the culture of time and place that a translator cannot find an exact equivalent in a new language. "Un honnête homme" is a good example. "Honnête" is cognate with the English "honest," which now usually suggests someone who tells the truth. But in seventeenth-century France the word had a much wider meaning: it implied probity, worthiness, decency, virtue (in the sense of chastity as well as general goodness), politeness and elegance, deep and discreet intelligence, moral stature without prudishness, and a position in society that reflected good standing. How does one translate such a term without using all these and perhaps other synonyms?

Added to the difficulty of carrying meaning across three centuries and an ocean is the problem that in Molière's plays a word is often embedded in an Alexandrine couplet, whose exigencies of hexameter and rhyme can push the author to word choices and arrangements that might not have been used in prose. A look at the catalogue of any library under the heading "Molière" will show that many translators have set themselves to what seems like an impossible task, and that many have in fact succeeded in their efforts. This translation appears in a long line of such efforts, which began in the late seventeenth century and which will continue as long as readers want to see themselves through the lenses of another world.

Two elements may be of interest to these readers. The first appears in Act I, scene 2. Oronte, an ambitious man, comes to

Translator's Note: *The Misanthrope*

visit Alceste—the misanthrope—and his friend Philinte. He asks Alceste to comment on a sonnet he has written. Alceste declines: "One of my faults is to be a little more candid than necessary." Oronte insists on reading, and, having listened to the arch and artificial first lines, Philinte comments, "I'm already astounded by this first little bit." In the French Molière has Philinte describe himself as *charmé*—"spellbound," "charmed," "delighted" are standard translations. From "spellbound" to "astounded" is not much of a jump; why choose "astounded"? Because today "astounded" has an ambiguous meaning: it can mean delighted, of course, and it can also mean shocked. Philinte is Molière's representative of good sense, of moderation. Caught between good manners and loyalty to his friend Alceste, he might well take refuge in ambiguity, especially since in the first scene he has criticized Alceste's blunt and aggressive intention to challenge and defy the whole human race.

Oronte's verses present their own challenge. Arch and artificial, imitative of the worst mannered style of the seventeenth-century *Précieuses* poets, the meter and the rhyme patterns of the original seemed worth evoking even though translating the exact words in their original order is impossible. For readers who would like to make the direct comparison, the original text appears in the Notes to *The Misanthrope*.

A second set of choices comes in Act V, scenes 2 and 3. Once again Alceste and Oronte confront each other, this time vying for the love of Célimène. Molière, a master of stagecraft as well as of poetry, sets the rivals in a physical triangle with Célimène at the apex. Each is persuaded that he is her beloved; both, being men of manners, wish to seem fair-minded. At the beginning of both scenes, each is given standard Alexandrine speeches. But as the men's tempers rise, Molière uses a device that first appeared in the theater of classical Athens. The technical term is *stichomythia*—each character speaks one line that rhymes with the line that the previous character has said. The alternation of voices, the abruptness of the single lines linked by rhyme, adds a particular force to the exchanges. This translation has echoed

Translator's Note: *The Misanthrope*

Molière's device, partly to add a comic tension to the scenes, partly to give today's reader a more immediate sense of how the play was heard when it was first performed in 1666.

Translators and commentators are always in debt to others. I am grateful to my first French teacher, the late Mlle. Marie Schaffter Bruggère; my teachers at Reid Hall in Paris in 1953; the late Professor Herbert Dieckmann of Harvard University; Dr. Pamela S. Green; and Professor Robert Jouanny, whose notes to the Garnier edition of Molière's plays have been of the greatest value.

The Misanthrope

Cast of Characters

ALCESTE, in love with Célimène
PHILINTE, friend of Alceste
ORONTE, suitor of Célimène
CÉLIMÈNE, beloved of Alceste
ÉLIANTE, cousin of Célimène
ARSINOÉ, friend of Célimène
ACASTE, a marquis
CLITANDRE, a marquis
BASQUE, valet of Célimène
A GUARD of the mounted police
DU BOIS, valet of Alceste[1]

The scene is set in Paris.

---

1. See the note on the names of the characters on pages 233–34.

Act I

Scene 1

PHILINTE, ALCESTE

Philinte
What's this? What's the matter with you?

Alceste
Please—leave me.

Philinte
Come on, tell me what this strange behavior . . .

Alceste
Leave me alone, run away, disappear.

Philinte
You should at least listen to people without being angry.

Alceste
I want to be angry, and I don't want to listen.

The Misanthrope, Act I, scene 1

Philinte
I can never understand you when you're suddenly in one of these moods, and even though we're friends, I'm always the first . . .

Alceste
I—your friend? Scratch me off the list. I may have said I was, but after what I just saw I'm telling you straight off that I'm not your friend any longer. I don't want to be loved by anyone who's so corrupt.

Philinte
Then by your standards, Alceste, I'm a sinner?

Alceste
You—you should be dying of shame. Your behavior is inexcusable; any honorable man would be scandalized by it. I saw you overwhelming a man with affection, protesting loyalty, making offers and promises, smothering him with a hug; and when I asked you who that man was, you scarcely knew his name. You cooled off the moment you left him, and you claimed he's of no interest to you. Damn! That's shameful, cowardly, appalling. You betray your soul when you stoop so low. If by some misfortune I had done what you did I'd hang myself in a moment, out of sheer remorse.

Philinte
I myself don't see that this is a hanging offense. Remit my sentence, I implore you; don't hang me for what I did.

Alceste
That joke is in bad taste.

Philinte
But seriously, what do you want people to do?

The Misanthrope, Act I, scene 1

Alceste
I want people to be sincere. An honorable man should never say anything that he doesn't truly believe.

Philinte
When someone greets you enthusiastically, I think one should return the favor; respond in kind, as much as possible. If he makes offers or promises, do the same for him.

Alceste
No, I can't bear the despicable behavior I see in most of you fashionable gentlemen. I abhor the contortions made by those effusive fellows who shower affable and meaningless embraces on everyone, who pleasantly talk about nothing, who are at odds with everyone in the most civil terms, and treat the honorable and the worthless exactly the same way. What good is it when a man embraces you, swears friendship, faith, zeal, respect, praises you to the skies, if he does the same for any fool? No, no decent man wants to be honored by someone who prostitutes himself that way; the highest compliments are worthless if they're paid to all and sundry. Esteem is based on careful judgment; those who value everyone value no one. Since you behave this way, by Heaven, you're not one of my friends; I don't want to have anything to do with an amiable soul who's unwilling to discriminate among people. I want to be different; and to be blunt, the man who's everyone's friend is no friend of mine.

Philinte
But when you live in the world you have to behave civilly, the way the world expects.

Alceste
No: I tell you we should condemn without mercy this disgraceful trade in false friendship. We should be men, and every time we meet someone we should show what we really

are; our hearts should speak and our feelings should never hide behind false compliments.

Philinte
There are lots of places where frankness would seem ridiculous—and unacceptable; sometimes, if I may say so without offending your rigid sense of honor, it's as well to hide one's opinions. Would it be appropriate, good manners, to tell everyone what we think of them? And if there's someone whom we hate, or dislike, should we tell him so point-blank?

Alceste
Yes.

Philinte
What? Would you go tell old Émilie that at her age it's a mistake to pretend to be a pretty young thing, and that all her makeup scandalizes everyone?

Alceste
Certainly.

Philinte
Would you tell Dorilas that he's too pushy, that everyone at Court is bored by the way he boasts about his courage and his good family?

Alceste
Absolutely.

Philinte
You're joking.

Alceste
I'm not joking. I won't spare anyone. I am disgusted; all I see in the Court and the city are things that enrage me. I'm in a black

mood, I'm appalled when I see how human beings behave in society: there's nothing but cowardly flattery, injustice, self-interest, treason, deceit. I can't stop; I'm furious; I intend to challenge and defy the whole human race.

Philinte
This savage philosophy goes a bit too far; I can only chuckle when I see your black mood. When I look at the two of us—both of us brought up the same way—I feel that I'm watching the two brothers in Molière's play *The School for Husbands,* about whom . . .[1]

Alceste
Good Lord! Stop all these shabby comparisons.

Philinte
Stop all these outbursts. Your efforts won't change the world. And since you find candor so attractive, I'll tell you candidly that people everywhere laugh at your bad moods; your attacks on the way we live now simply make you look ridiculous.

Alceste
So much the better, damn it! So much the better: that's just what I hope for; it's a good omen, I'm delighted by it. I find everyone so odious that their good opinion would horrify me.

Philinte
So you want to condemn all humanity?

Alceste
Yes, I hate it, intensely.

---

1. Molière's play concerns two brothers who are, in temperament, somewhat like Alceste and Philinte.

The Misanthrope, Act I, scene 1

Philinte
You hate all poor mortals, without any exceptions? Might there be some in this century . . .

Alceste
No: impossible; I hate them all. Some of them because they are wicked and malicious; others because they are complacent about the wicked and don't hate them the way virtuous people should hate vice. The results of this complicity? Look at the scoundrel who brought a case against me. Look at that traitor peering through his mask. He's recognized everywhere for what he is; but even though he rolls his eyes and speaks pleasantly, he deceives only the people who've never met him before. Everyone grants that he's an oaf who ought to be challenged, who's pushed himself into society in an underhanded way that makes decent men wince and blush. Everyone knows his shameful reputation, and nobody takes his side. Call him a cheat, a despicable, damned scoundrel: everyone will agree, no one will contradict you. And yet he smirks and sneaks in everywhere, everyone welcomes him and laughs at his jokes; and if there is some position that intrigue can get for him, he is appointed instead of a more honest man. Damnation! Such things cut me to the quick; sometimes I feel I must escape to some remote place, away from all human beings.

Philinte
Come, come — don't be so upset by today's customs; let's be a bit more generous, more tolerant of the flaws in human nature, and not examine it too rigorously. We need a somewhat flexible virtue when we're out in the world; too much austerity leaves us open to criticism. In fact, being truly reasonable means avoiding extremes; yes, we must be virtuous — in moderation. Old-fashioned rectitude seems out of place these days; it demands too much perfection of us mortals. We can't be obstinate, we have to bend with the times, and it's pure folly

The Misanthrope, Act I, scene 1

to try to correct everyone's behavior. Every day I see what you see—a hundred things that could be better, could be done differently; but even though such things happen everywhere, no one sees me raging about them. I'm willing to take men as they are; I train myself to put up with what they do; and I think that, whether you're at Court or in town, being cool is as reasonable as being hot headed.

Alceste
But this cool, easy-going temperament, Monsieur, couldn't something make it erupt? If, for example, a friend should betray you; if someone concocts a scheme to grab what's yours, if someone starts to spread vile rumors about you, would you take all this calmly and coolly?

Philinte
Oh, I see all these bad things you complain about—those vices are part of human nature. But I'm no more offended by a knave, a cheat, a self-centered man than I am by vultures tearing at a carcass, or meddling monkeys, or rabid wolves.

Alceste
Must I see myself betrayed, torn apart, robbed, without being . . . Damn! Your arguments are too specious—I don't want to say another word.

Philinte
Heavens, yes! You ought to stop talking, and avoid attacking your opponent. You'd do better to pay more attention to your lawsuit.

Alceste
I won't: I've said so already.

Philinte
But whom will you ask to argue on your behalf?

Alceste
Whom? Reason, my rights, equity.

Philinte
You won't go to call on the judges?

Alceste
No. Is my lawsuit unjust, or in doubt?

Philinte
Of course not; but the faction against you is troublesome, and . . .

Alceste
No: I've decided not to lift a finger. Either I'm wrong, or I'm right.

Philinte
Don't count on it.

Alceste
I will not budge.

Philinte
Your opponent is strong, and could use his cabal to drag . . .

Alceste
No matter.

Philinte
You would be making a mistake.

Alceste
So be it. I want to see how it all comes out.

Philinte
But . . .

The Misanthrope, Act I, scene 1

Alceste
I'll have the pleasure of losing the case.

Philinte
But in the end . . .

Alceste
I'll see, during the trial, whether those men have enough gall, are wicked, conniving, and corrupt enough to perpetrate an injustice that all the world would recognize.

Philinte
What a man!

Alceste
Even if it costs me a fortune, I'm willing to lose the case just for the satisfaction of it.

Philinte
People would laugh at you, Alceste, if they heard you talk this way.

Alceste
Too bad for them.

Philinte
But this moral rectitude about which you're so punctilious, this virtue in which you wrap yourself, do you see it in the woman you love? Since you and the odious human race are so much at odds (or so it seems), I'm surprised that you could find anyone to enchant you; and I'm even more surprised by the person you've chosen. You've rejected truehearted Éliante, who is attracted to you; and prudish Arsinoé, who eyes you longingly. But you've been captivated by that flirt Célimène, whose cutting wit seems to reflect the manners of the times. You despise that kind of behavior; how can you put up with it in

this pretty woman? Isn't it a defect in your sweetheart? Don't you see it? Do you simply make excuses for it?

Alceste
No, the love I feel for this young widow doesn't make me blind to her defects. I'm the first to see them and condemn them, even though I adore her. I can't help it; I admit it: I'm weak; she is lovable. Her charms are stronger than I am; and besides, my devotion to her will surely purge her of these vices.

Philinte
That would be no small accomplishment! You think, then, that she loves you?

Alceste
Yes, certainly! I wouldn't love her if I didn't think I was loved.

Philinte
But if she's shown you that she favors you, why are you so irritated by your rivals?

Alceste
Because someone who's in love wants to have his beloved all to himself; I've come here precisely to tell her how I feel.

Philinte
Well, if it were up to me, I'd devote myself to Éliante. Her heart is steady and sincere, she admires you; you'd do better if you chose her.

Alceste
Yes, you're right; my mind tells me this every day, but the mind doesn't govern love.

Philinte
I'm worried about this passion; your hopes might be . . .

Scene 2

ORONTE, ALCESTE, PHILINTE

Oronte
I heard downstairs that Éliante and Célimène have gone shopping, but since I learned that you are here, I came up to tell you, with total sincerity, that I have unbelievable respect for you, and that for some time this respect has been growing into a passionate desire to be one of your friends. Yes, yes, my heart recognizes and values true merit, and I'm burning to unite us in the bond of friendship: I believe that an ardent friend of my stature is surely not something to be rejected. [*Here Alceste appears to be daydreaming and seems not to understand that Oronte is speaking to him.*]² Excuse me, Monsieur: I'm speaking to you.

Alceste
To me, Monsieur?

Oronte
To you. Does this shock you?

Alceste
No, but it is quite a surprise. I never expected such an honor.

---

2. Italicized stage directions come from Molière's text.

The Misanthrope, Act I, scene 2

Oronte
You should not be surprised by how much I esteem you—an esteem that is shared by the whole world.

Alceste
Monsieur . . .

Oronte
The nation has no honor great enough for your dazzling merit.

Alceste
Monsieur . . .

Oronte
Yes, I, for one, consider you more worthy of honors than all the most eminent men.

Alceste
Monsieur . . .

Oronte
May the heavens crush me if I lie! And to assure you of my feelings, please allow me to embrace you, Monsieur, with an open heart, and to claim a place in your list of friends. Shake my hand, please. You will promise? Your friendship?

Alceste
Monsieur . . .

Oronte
What? You hold back?

Alceste
Monsieur, you honor me too much. But friendship—that's a relationship that develops only slowly, cautiously; it's a serious mistake to apply the word loosely to any and every encounter.

The Misanthrope, Act I, scene 2

Before being linked as you request, we need to know one another better; we might discover that we're sufficiently different to regret our relationship.

Oronte
My word! There speaks a wise man; I value you all the more for what you've said. We'll let time bring us closer—and meanwhile, I pledge myself entirely at your service. If you need some introductions at Court, well, everyone knows that the King has some respect for me; he listens to me; his behavior with me, well! It's as courteous as one could wish! In short, I'm yours to command. And now, since you're known for your insight, I'll start off our relationship by showing you a sonnet that I just wrote, and asking you whether I should publish it.

Alceste
I'm ill-suited to judge such matters, Monsieur; pray excuse me.

Oronte
Why?

Alceste
One of my faults is to be a little more candid than necessary.

Oronte
That's just what I hoped, and, since I asked for your honest opinion, I would have reason to complain if you did not tell me the truth.

Alceste
Since this is what you wish, I will certainly do so.

Oronte
"Sonnet" . . . It is a sonnet. "Hope" . . . It is about a lady who, giving me some hope, had encouraged me. "Hope" . . . These are not lofty verses, but simple, gentle, sweet, seductive lines. [*Each time he pauses he looks at Alceste.*]

The Misanthrope, Act I, scene 2

Alceste
We shall see.

Oronte
"Hope" . . . I don't know whether the style will seem clear and easy enough, and whether you'll approve of my choice of words.

Alceste
We'll see soon enough, Monsieur.

Oronte
You understand, I spent only a quarter of an hour writing it.

Alceste
Come, Monsieur; the amount of time is irrelevant.

Oronte
> *Hope, it is true, calms emotions*
> *And frees us a time from our care.*
> *But Philis, what good are such notions,*
> *Since delay pushes me to despair?*

Philinte
I'm already astounded by this first little bit.

Alceste
What? Can you admire this with a straight face?

Oronte
> *Your kindness I used to receive,*
> *This kindness no longer is there,*
> *You should not have let me believe:*
> *My hopes must give way to despair.*

Philinte
This is the language of gallantry!

Alceste [*Under his breath.*]
Damn! You flatterer—can you praise such stupidity?

Oronte
> *Now all this frustration I feel*
> *Has finally conquered my zeal*
> *I've come to the end of my rope;*
>
> *No more can your exquisite charm*
> *Sustain me or keep me from harm:*
> *I cannot live solely on hope.*[3]

Philinte
The conclusion is tender, astonishing!

Alceste [*Under his breath.*]
Damn your conclusion. It's poisonous! It makes me want to box your ears!

Philinte
I've never heard such ingenious rhymes.

Alceste
Damn it!

Oronte
You're just flattering me, and perhaps you think . . .

Philinte
No, not flattering.

---

3. See the note on "Oronte's Sonnet" on pages 234–35.

The Misanthrope, Act I, scene 2

Alceste [*Under his breath.*]
Then what are you doing, traitor?

Oronte
Now, remember our agreement: tell me the truth.

Alceste
Monsieur, this is a delicate matter. One always wants to be told one has talent. Well, now, one day, seeing verses like these, I told the author—I won't say his name—that a gentleman must always control the itch to write; that he should rein in the urge to publish his trifles; and showing off one's work can lead one to play a ridiculous role.

Oronte
Do you mean by this that I'm wrong to . . .

Alceste
I didn't say that. But I told this person that mere mechanical skill is boring and a writer who has nothing more to offer is subject to scorn. Furthermore, even those with hundreds of talents are frequently attacked on their weakest side.

Oronte
Are you saying that about my sonnet?

Alceste
I didn't say that. But to discourage him from writing I pointed out that many good men nowadays have been harmed by their desire to publish.

Oronte
Do I write badly? Do I resemble such men?

Alceste
I didn't say that. But finally, I said to him, why is it so important to be a rhymester? And what in the world possessed you to publish? If we forgive bad books, it's only because poor

The Misanthrope, Act I, scene 2

devils had to write them to earn a living. Believe me: resist the temptation, hide these efforts from the public; no matter what you're offered, don't jeopardize your good reputation at Court just because a publisher offers you the opportunity of being called a foolish shabby writer. That's what I tried to make him understand.

Oronte
Quite right, and I think I understand you. But couldn't I learn what there is in my sonnet . . . ?

Alceste
Frankly, it would be better to leave it in your desk. You've chosen a bad model, and your turns of phrase are forced. What is "And frees us a time from our care"? And "Since delay pushes me to despair"? And "You should not have let me believe"? And "I cannot live solely on hope"? This elaborate style that people praise so much is a departure from honest feeling, from truth; it's nothing but a play on words, sheer affectation: human nature doesn't speak that way. Today's bad taste gives me the shivers. Our fathers, coarse as they were, had better taste. I'm less impressed by what is admired today than I am by an old song that I'll recite:

> *If King Henry were to say,*
> *"Paris shall be yours today,*
> *But you'll have to go away*
>   *From your true beloved,"*
>
> *I would tell King Henry then,*
> *"Take your Paris back again.*
> *I prefer my one true love,*
>   *I love my beloved."*[4]

---

4. See the note on "If King Henry . . . " on page 235 for the original text and the music. One report indicates that Molière, who played the part of Alceste, first sang the verses and later recited them.

The Misanthrope, Act I, scene 2

The rhyme is simple and the style old-fashioned, but can't you see that it's worth much more than these frilly pieces that good sense condemns? Don't you see that passion speaks more clearly here?

> *If King Henry were to say,*
> *"Paris shall be yours today,*
> *But you'll have to go away*
>   *From your true beloved,"*

> *I would tell King Henry then,*
> *"Take your Paris back again.*
> *I prefer my one true love,*
>   *I love my beloved."*

This is what a true lover would say. [*To Philinte.*] Yes, Monsieur, you're chuckling: well, I like this song better than the elaborate pomposity, those artificial diamonds that everyone praises.

Oronte
Well, I insist that my poetry is very good.

Alceste
You have your reasons to think so; and you will allow me to have mine, which must be excused from yielding to yours.

Oronte
All you need to know is that others admire it.

Alceste
That may be because they know how to pretend and I do not.

Oronte
Do you think you are so clever, then?

Alceste
No doubt I'd have to be to manufacture praise for your verses.

The Misanthrope, Act I, scene 2

Oronte
I'll manage to do without your praise.

Alceste
Yes, indeed, you will.

Oronte
I'd like to see the verses you could write on this subject.

Alceste
Alas, I could surely do as badly; but I'd keep myself from showing the results to others.

Oronte
Those are strong words, and your pride . . .

Alceste
You'll have to look for compliments elsewhere.

Oronte
My dear little fellow, let's not take that tone.

Alceste
My high and mighty fellow, I'll take whatever tone I want.

Philinte [*Coming between them.*]
Come, come, gentlemen; please, let's stop all this.

Oronte
Oh! I admit I'm in the wrong, and I'm leaving. Your servant, Monsieur, with all my heart.

Alceste
And I am yours, most humbly, Monsieur.

Scene 3

PHILINTE, ALCESTE

Philinte
Well! You see? By being too sincere you've got a quarrel on your hands. I could clearly see that Oronte, in order to hear something flattering . . .[5]

Alceste
Don't speak to me.

Philinte
But . . .

Alceste
Go away.

Philinte
It's too much . . .

Alceste
Leave me alone.

---

5. This episode, in a much compressed form, appears in Wycherley's *The Plain Dealer* (1674), Act III, scene 1, a play that is in part taken from *The Misanthrope*.

The Misanthrope, Act I, scene 3

Philinte
If I . . .

Alceste
Stop jabbering.

Philinte
But what? . . .

Alceste
I'm not listening.

Philinte
But . . .

Alceste
Still talking?

Philinte
You insult . . .

Alceste
Damn it! I've had enough. Stop following me.

Philinte
Don't be silly; I'm not leaving you.

Act II

Scene 1

ALCESTE, CÉLIMÈNE

Alceste
Madame, may I speak bluntly? I dislike your behavior. It offends me; it makes me think we will have to leave one another. Yes, I'd be lying if I said anything else; sooner or later, we'll surely separate. Even if I promised a thousand times that this wouldn't happen, I'd be powerless to prevent it.

Célimène
Am I right to think that you offered to escort me home simply to quarrel with me?

Alceste
I'm not quarrelling with you, Madame; I'm objecting to your willingness to make yourself accessible to all and sundry. You're preoccupied by those followers and I cannot put up with that.

The Misanthrope, Act II, scene 1

Célimène
Are you finding fault with me because of all those followers? Can I prevent people from liking me? And since they make such gallant efforts to visit me, should I take a stick and beat them away from the door?

Alceste
No, you do not need a stick, Madame; you need a heart that's less receptive to them. You enchant everyone wherever you go; when you welcome those who catch your eye, they instantly become your captives. And when you treat your slaves so sweetly you simply strengthen the spell. You encourage them to hope; well, that simply makes them more eager. If you were a little less obliging, you'd be rid of all this rabble. Now tell me, Madame, about Clitandre: how was he lucky enough to please you so much? What is his intrinsic merit, the sublime virtue that caused you to have such a high regard for him? Is it because of that long fingernail on his little finger that he has a hold on you? Have you succumbed—like all the fashionable people—to his ravishing blond wig? Did his huge breeches prompt you to love him? That heap of ribbons, his elegant boot-tops—did they enslave you? Or his falsetto laugh—is that his secret weapon?[6]

Célimène
How unfairly you attack him! Don't you understand why I encourage him? He promises to use his friends to help me in the lawsuit I'm involved in.[7]

Alceste
Lose your lawsuit, Madame, and be firm; don't entangle yourself with a rival who offends me.

---

6. This speech has its echo in Wycherley's *The Plain Dealer*, Act II, scene 1.
7. See the note on "Lawsuits in *The Misanthrope*" on pages 236–37. The frontispiece shows something of Clitandre's appearance.

The Misanthrope, Act II, scene 1

Célimène
You seem to be jealous of everyone on earth.

Alceste
That's because you welcome everyone on earth.

Célimène
The fact that I treat everyone the same way should reassure you. You would have more cause to complain if I paid special attention to only one person.

Alceste
You accuse me of being jealous, but what advantage do I have over the others?

Célimène
The happiness of knowing that you are loved.

Alceste
What's the evidence that this is true?

Célimène
My having taken the trouble to tell you so. Such an admission ought to be enough.

Alceste
And how can I be sure that you don't say the same thing to everyone?

Célimène
What a lovely bouquet to give the person you love. You talk to me just as if I were an honorable woman. Well, to end your doubts, I'll deny everything I just said; now the only one who can deceive you is yourself. Be satisfied with that.

The Misanthrope, Act II, scene 1

Alceste
Damn it! Why do I have to love you! Oh! If I could tear myself away from you, how I'd thank Heaven! It's true: I do my best to break out of this terrible obsession, but each time I fail. For my sins I'm condemned to love you.

Célimène
True: your passion for me is unique.

Alceste
Yes, on that point I'll challenge anyone. No one can imagine how much I love; no one, Madame, has ever loved as I do.

Célimène
Yes, indeed, it's an entirely original way of courting, for you love people simply in order to quarrel with them. Your passion is ruthless; never has a lover been such a scold.

Alceste
But you could so easily make me feel better. Let's abandon these quarrels, let's talk with open hearts, and let's stop . . .

Scene 2

Célimène, Alceste, Basque

Célimène
What is it?

Basque
Acaste is here.

Célimène
Well, ask him to come up.

Alceste
What? Can one never be alone with you? Are you always ready to receive visitors? Couldn't you, just once, say that you are not at home?

Célimène
Do you want me to insult him?

Alceste
Your relations with him displease me.

Célimène
He's a man who would never forgive me if he thought that I found his company disagreeable.

The Misanthrope, Act II, scene 2

Alceste
And why do you burden yourself this way?

Célimène
Oh, Heavens! The goodwill of his friends is important; somehow they have the ear of the Court, and they insert themselves into every conversation. It's true that they cannot help, but they certainly can harm. No matter what other support one may have, one should not offend these quarrelsome people.

Alceste
Well, no matter when or why, you find a way to welcome everyone; the warnings that your good sense . . .

Scene 3

BASQUE, ALCESTE, CÉLIMÈNE

Basque
Clitandre has also come, Madame.

Alceste [*He seems to want to leave.*]
Exactly.

Célimène
Where are you going?

Alceste
I'm leaving.

Célimène
Stay.

Alceste
Why?

Célimène
Stay.

Alceste
I cannot.

The Misanthrope, Act II, scene 3

Célimène
I want you to.

Alceste
None of that. These conversations only annoy me, and you're asking too much of me.

Célimène
You must, you must stay.

Alceste
No, that's impossible.

Célimène
Well, then, leave; you have a perfect right to go.

Scene 4

Éliante, Philinte, Acaste,
Clitandre, Alceste,
Célimène, Basque

Éliante
The two marquis are coming up with us; did someone tell you?

Célimène
Yes—bring chairs for everyone. [*To Alceste.*] You haven't left?

Alceste
No; and I want you, Madame, to say where you stand—either with them or with me.

Célimène
Do be quiet.

Alceste
Right now: make things clear.

Célimène
You have lost your wits.

Alceste
Not at all. Announce your intentions.

The Misanthrope, Act II, scene 4

Célimène
Ah!

Alceste
You must choose.

Célimène
You're joking, I assume.

Alceste
No; you must choose; I've been patient long enough.

Clitandre
By Jove! I've just come from the Louvre, where Cléonte, at the King's reception,[8] made a perfect fool of himself, Madame. Doesn't he have a friend who could kindly give him some hints about his manners?

Célimène
It's quite true, he does make a mess of things in society. He's awkward; he attracts attention; in fact, he seems more outlandish each time one sees him.

Acaste
Well, now, if we're talking about outlandish people, I've just had to put up with one of the worst: Damon the disputatious, who kept me standing in front of my carriage for a whole hour, in the hot sun.

Célimène
He is an odd preachy fellow, and he's perfected the art of making long speeches that always manage to convey nothing at all. There's not a drop of sense in anything he says; when you listen to him, all you hear is noise.

---

8. Clitandre uses the word "levé," usually translated as "levee"—a morning reception—which meant literally "the rising of the king."

Éliante [*To Philinte.*]
As attacks on others go, these are quite promising.

Clitandre
Timante, now, is a good fellow, Madame.

Célimène
There's a man of mystery, from head to toe. When he walks by he gives you a wild look, and even though he has nothing to do, he always looks busy. He makes faces when he talks, and his mannerisms bore everyone. He is always interrupting to murmur a secret—a secret of no importance whatever, a trifle that he thinks is astonishing; even when he says "good morning" he whispers like a conspirator.

Acaste
And Géralde, Madame?

Célimène
Oh, what a bore! He's forever pretending to be a great nobleman. He always moves in high society—all he ever mentions is a duke, a prince, a princess, horses, carriages, dogs. He's fixated on aristocracy; he's on intimate terms with the elite, and no one has ever heard him address someone as an ordinary "*Mister* So and So."

Clitandre
They say that he and Bélise are very close.

Célimène
That dreary woman! What a dry stick she is! I'm in agony when she comes to call. Finding something to say is like pulling teeth; any one of her tedious comments stops all further conversation. Even the ordinary topics are useless: good weather, bad, rain, heat, cold—none of these seems to interest her. And her tiresome visits drag on and on and on. You can ask what time it is, yawn—she's as motionless as a block of wood.

The Misanthrope, Act II, scene 4

Acaste
What do you think of Adraste?

Célimène
What outrageous pride! He's swollen with self-love. He complains that the Court does not appreciate him; he bustles about there every day, and when someone else receives an appointment or a position, then, according to him, he is being treated unfairly.

Clitandre
Now, young Cléon, whom all the best people visit—what can you say about him?

Célimène
It is his cook and his dining table that people visit.

Éliante
He certainly serves delicious meals.

Célimène
Yes, but I wish he'd serve less of himself. He's a tasteless mess, and as far as I'm concerned, he spoils every dinner that he offers.

Philinte
People speak highly of his uncle Damis: what do you say, Madame?

Célimène
He is one of my friends.

Philinte
He is an honorable, decent man, and seems to be wise.

The Misanthrope, Act II, scene 4

Célimène
Yes. But he tries too hard to be witty, and that infuriates me. He ties himself into knots to be clever, and everything he says is an effort to be brilliant. Since he decided that he's a perceptive fellow, he's perpetually dissatisfied and demanding. He finds fault with everything he reads. He believes that praising something shows a lack of taste; that the wise always censure; that only fools admire and can be amused. And he thinks that if he condemns everything written today, that shows he's better than everyone. Even in a conversation he sneers, as if it would be beneath him to reply. He simply stands there, folds his arms, and squints down his nose as if he's taking pity on everyone else.

Acaste
Bless me, there's his portrait to a T.

Clitandre
You're an admirable painter![9]

Alceste
Right, that's quite enough, my dear courtiers. You spare no one, each is condemned; yet as soon as someone approaches you, you rush to meet him, shake his hand, give him a flattering embrace, swear you are his obedient servant.

Clitandre
Why are you angry at us? If you're offended by what we say, you should be telling this to Madame.

Alceste
No, damn it! It's your fault. When you laugh tolerantly you just encourage these nasty remarks. You pander to her taste for satire; she'd be less likely to mock if she saw that she wasn't

---

9. Wycherley echoes this scene in *The Plain Dealer*, Act II, scene 1.

being praised for it. That's why we should reject flattery: it's the cause of humanity's bad habits.

Philinte
But why are you defending these people, since you yourself attack them for the same faults?

Célimène
But it is necessary for Monsieur to contradict. Do you want him to agree with what everyone says? Heaven made him a contrarian, and therefore he must erupt. He can't possibly be pleased with something that pleases others. He's obliged to be on the opposite side of any question, and he would think himself worthless if he agreed with someone. He so enjoys disagreeing that sometimes he has to disagree with himself, and he'll even object to his own opinions if someone else shares them.

Alceste
These witty men are on your side, Madame; go on: be satirical at my expense.

Philinte
But it's also the case that you attack everything that others say, and your bitterness—which even you recognize—won't permit anyone else to condemn or praise.

Alceste
Since, damn it, men are always wrong, my anger is always appropriate. No matter where I look, all I see is dishonest praise or malicious criticism.

Célimène
But . . .

The Misanthrope, Act II, scene 4

Alceste
No, Madame, no. I'd rather die than put up with some of the things that please you. People are wrong to encourage you to speak as you do—and some of them even criticize you for such unworthy behavior.

Clitandre
I don't know . . . but I admit aloud that I've always believed that Madame is flawless.

Acaste
I see her full of grace and charm; any defects are invisible, to me.

Alceste
I see them all too well, and rather than pretending that I don't, I take care to show them to her, as she knows. The more one loves, the less may one flatter. Pure love shines most when it pardons least. For my part, I would chase away all those cowardly suitors who agree with everything I said, whose spineless affability would only encourage my folly.

Célimène
Then, if all hearts must be like yours, a true lover should stop being kind and, out of pure love, insult his beloved.

Éliante
Love doesn't ordinarily follow such rules; lovers always boast about those they love. They never see anything wrong with their beloved—for them, everything is adorable. They see defects as perfections and know how to find the right words for them. If the lady is pale, she is as white as jasmine; if she's dreadfully swarthy, she's called an enchanting brunette. Gaunt? No: she has a beautiful supple figure; fat: she's majestic. A slovenly graceless person is called an artless beauty. You say too tall? Not a bit: she looks like a goddess. A dwarf?

The Misanthrope, Act II, scene 4

Well, she's a tiny storehouse of virtues. Proud? She's worthy of a crown. A trickster is witty, a fool is all goodness, a chatterbox is full of good humor, and someone who doesn't speak is honorably modest. That's how an adoring lover describes the flaws of someone he loves.[10]

Alceste
And I, I insist . . .

Célimène
Shall we end this conversation and walk a bit in the gallery? Oh? You gentlemen are leaving?

Clitandre and **Acaste**
Not at all, Madame.

Alceste
You seem very much afraid that they will leave. Leave when you wish, gentlemen; but I warn you that I will not leave until after you do.

Acaste
Nothing prevents me from staying all day, unless Madame finds me a nuisance.

Clitandre
As for me, as long as I can be at the last reception of the evening, nothing else claims my attention.

Célimène
I assume all this is a joke.

Alceste
Not at all. We'll see whether it's I whom you're asking to leave.

---

10. See the note on "Éliante's speech" on pages 237–38.

Scene 5

BASQUE, ALCESTE,
CÉLIMÈNE, ÉLIANTE, ACASTE,
PHILINTE, CLITANDRE

Basque
Sir, a man has come who wants to see you on a matter that can't be put off.

Alceste
Tell him that I'm not engaged in any matters that are so urgent.

Basque
He is wearing a very large jacket with huge stripes, with gold stuff on it.

Célimène
Go ask what it's about, or else have him come in.

Alceste
What in the world do you want? Come in, Monsieur.

Scene 6

GUARD, ALCESTE, CÉLIMÈNE,
ÉLIANTE, ACASTE,
PHILINTE, CLITANDRE

Guard
Monsieur, I have a few words for you.

Alceste
Speak up, Monsieur, and let me hear them.

Guard
The Marshals, whose orders I obey, require you to come immediately, Monsieur.

Alceste
Who, me?

Guard
You yourself.

Alceste
For what reason?

Philinte
It's because of this ridiculous business with Oronte.

The Misanthrope, Act II, scene 6

Célimène
What's that?

Philinte
A little while ago Oronte and he challenged one another because of some verses that Alceste didn't like; this is an attempt to stop it all before it goes farther.

Alceste
I would never be so cowardly as to withdraw.

Philinte
But we must obey the order; come, get ready . . .

Alceste
How could this possibly be resolved amicably? Would these officials condemn me to like the verses at the heart of our dispute? I won't retract what I said: the verses are miserable.

Philinte
But a more gentle . . .

Alceste
I won't give up: the verses are execrable.

Philinte
You should express yourself differently; come on, let's go.

Alceste
I'll go, but nothing will force me to retract.

Philinte
Let's go so that you can present yourself.

Alceste
Unless the King himself ordered me to approve these verses about which there's such a fuss, I will continue to insist, damn

it! that they are terrible; and that the man who could write them deserves to be hanged. [*To Clitandre and Acaste, who are laughing.*] My word, gentlemen, I didn't realize I was so witty.

Célimène
Hurry off to wherever you're supposed to appear.

Alceste
I am going, Madame, and will return promptly to settle our dispute.

Act III

Scene 1

CLITANDRE, ACASTE

Clitandre
Dear Marquis, you look very pleased with yourself. Everything delights you, nothing worries you. Tell the truth: do you really believe that you have good reasons to be so happy?

Acaste
Heavens! When I examine myself, I see no reason at all to be miserable. I'm wealthy, young, the son of a good family that could properly call itself noble; and thanks to my rank and my lineage, I think that there are very few positions that I'm not equipped to fill. As for my courage, which of course we must take very seriously, everyone knows that I—speaking without vanity—don't lack that. Many people have seen me undertake a duel gallantly and energetically. I'm witty, of course, and even without studying I have such good taste that my opinions are always correct, and I can defend them fluently. I adore novelty, and when I'm at the theater I'm the perfect critic;

The Misanthrope, Act III, scene 1

I'm always the first to cheer wildly at all the best parts. I'm quite clever; carry myself well: handsome, just the right size, especially good teeth. When it comes to being well dressed, I think—without flattering myself—that no one can challenge me. I'm very highly esteemed; loved by the fair sex, and in good standing with the husbands. Given all this, dear Marquis, I think that anyone anywhere could justifiably be self-satisfied.

Clitandre
Yes, to be sure; but having made easy conquests elsewhere, why are you here sighing for what you cannot have?

Acaste
I? My word, I'm not a man to put up with a frigid beauty. It's all very well for awkward, ordinary men to burn with love for a heartless woman, to languish at her feet, tolerate her whims, weep and sigh to advance their case, and after countless efforts, try to obtain what they don't deserve. Men like me, Marquis, do not give love on credit and bear all the expense, however beautiful a woman may be. I think that I am, thank God, as valuable as she; if a woman wants the honor of my love, there's no reason that she shouldn't pay for it. In sum, I think that making progress in love means defraying the costs equally.

Clitandre
Then you think your position here is good?

Acaste
I have some reason to think so.

Clitandre
Believe me: you should abandon this grotesque mistake. You're just flattering and blinding yourself.

Acaste
You're right, I flatter and blind myself.

Clitandre
But what persuades you that your happiness is assured?

Acaste
I flatter myself.

Clitandre
What are your hopes based on?

Acaste
I blind myself.

Clitandre
Have you evidence to support you?

Acaste
I'm deceiving myself, as I said.

Clitandre
Has Célimène secretly admitted her desire?

Acaste
No, I'm treated very badly.

Clitandre
Come on, please answer me.

Acaste
I've had only rejection.

Clitandre
Stop joking, and tell me what hope you've been given.

Acaste
I'm the one who's miserable, and you're the lucky man. She can't stand me, and one day, I'll have to hang myself.

The Misanthrope, Act III, scene 1

Clitandre
Oh, come on . . . Let's straighten this out, Marquis. Would you be willing to make a pact? If one of us can prove definitely that he's won Célimène's heart, the other will surrender the field to the man who claims victory and free him from his rival.

Acaste
Oh, by Jove, that's a splendid plan and I'll willingly agree to it. But shh!

Scene 2

Célimène, Acaste, Clitandre

Célimène
Still here?

Clitandre
Love keeps us here.

Célimène
I heard a coach below; do you know who is coming?

Scene 3

BASQUE, CÉLIMÈNE,
ACASTE, CLITANDRE

Basque
Madame, Arsinoé is coming up to see you.

Célimène
What does that woman want with me?

Basque
Éliante is keeping her company downstairs.

Célimène
What can she be thinking of, and who sent her?

Acaste
She's a perfect prude, as everyone knows, and she's so intense about it . . .

Célimène
Yes, yes, what a phony! The truth is, she's a worldly person who's forever trying to snare a man—without success. She's always looking enviously at the lovers who have devoted themselves to someone else; and when no one pays attention to her, this frustrated grouch complains about our wicked society that's blind to her virtue. She hides her frightful loneliness

The Misanthrope, Act III, scene 3

under the veil of propriety; and in self-defense she insists that it's sinful to be charming. But she'd love to have a lover, and she seems to have a weakness for Alceste. The fact that he pays attention to me outrages her; she claims that I've stolen him from her. She can barely hide her jealousy and spite, and she's ready to attack me, always and everywhere. Well, I've never seen anyone so stupid—to my way of thinking she's always a nuisance, and . . .

Scene 4

ARSINOÉ, CÉLIMÈNE

Célimène
Ah! What good wind blew you in here? I must tell you, frankly, Madame, that I was beginning to worry about you.

Arsinoé
I came with some news that I thought you should know.

Célimène
Oh, Lord! How happy I am to see you![11]

Arsinoé
Their departure couldn't be better timed.

Célimène
Shall we sit down?

Arsinoé
No need, Madame. Friendship is best demonstrated in times of need, and everyone needs a reputation for honor and propriety. That's why I've come: to demonstrate what a good friend I am by telling you something that bears on your honor. Yesterday I was with some people well known for their remarkable virtue,

---

11. Acaste and Clitandre leave.

The Misanthrope, Act III, scene 4

who were talking about you. And I must say, Madame, that your notorious behavior was much criticized. That crowd of visitors whom you welcome, your flirtations, provoke rumors; and the rumors have encouraged a larger number of harsh comments than one might need or want. You can imagine whose side I took; I did what I could to defend you. I made excuses for you and tried to testify on your behalf. But as you know, there are some things in life that one cannot excuse, no matter how much one would like to. I was forced to admit that your behavior injures your reputation. Some find it disreputable, others repeat all kinds of nasty tales. In short, they agreed that your manners might be less open to censure if you were to behave differently. Not that I believe that your honor has really been corrupted: Heaven forbid that I should think that! But people do take seriously even a hint of misconduct, and living simply to please oneself is not good enough. I think, Madame, that you are a reasonable person who will profit from this warning, since it is prompted by my devotion to your welfare.

Célimène
Madame, I owe you many thanks. This report is helpful, and far from taking it badly, I'll acknowledge the service you've done me by saying a word about something that concerns your own reputation. Since you've shown yourself to be my friend by reporting what's being said of me, I will follow your good example and report what others are saying about you. I was out, the other day, visiting some very admirable people, who, describing the good works of a virtuous person, turned the conversation toward you, Madame. Your prudishness and your zealotry, your affectation of sobriety, your endless sermons on good behavior and honor, your winces and little shrieks at the slightest shadows of indecency lurking in an innocent word, your lofty opinion of yourself, those pitying looks you give everyone, your repeated lessons, your censure of behavior that is perfectly decent and pure—all that, Madame, was

universally condemned. What, they said, is the point of that prim and proper appearance when everything else contradicts it? She may say her prayers meticulously, but she beats her servants and fails to pay them. She eagerly keeps company with the pious—but she wears makeup and does her best to look attractive. She covers painted scenes of nude figures, but she's quite fond of the real thing. I, of course, defended you against them all and assured them that this was just slander; but everyone there was against me, and they concluded that you would do better to stop worrying about the behavior of others and pay a bit more attention to your own. One has to look at oneself long and hard before condemning someone else, they said; only a person who has led an exemplary life should presume to criticize; and it's better to leave such tasks to those whom Heaven has chosen for this work. I'm sure, Madame, that you are so reasonable that you will profit from this warning and recognize that it is prompted by my zeal for your welfare.

Arsinoé
Though one may be forced to accept rebuke, I did not expect, Madame, such a response. Its sharpness makes me think that my well-intentioned advice has touched a nerve.

Célimène
Not at all, Madame; and if we were wise these mutual warnings would be more common. Spoken in good faith, they would put an end to one's blindness about oneself. If you will, we can continue to help each other this way, taking care to report what each of us has heard—you of me, I of you.

Arsinoé
Oh, Madame, I cannot imagine hearing anything about you; it's I who am subject to criticism.

The Misanthrope, Act III, scene 4

Célimène
Madame, anything can be praised or blamed, depending on the times and the customs. There's a time for flirtation, a time for prudishness. It makes good sense to be prim once our youthful charms have faded—doing so could help us avoid some annoying embarrassment. I don't deny that one day I may copy you; age brings changes, but it makes no sense to play the prude when one is twenty.

Arsinoé
I must say that when you boast about your youth you're making much of a rather trivial advantage. The fact that someone might be older than you isn't so significant; and I fail to see, Madame, why you attack me so harshly.

Célimène
And I, Madame, do not understand why you insult me everywhere you go. Do you have to scold me because of your own troubles? Can I avoid the attention that you don't receive? If people love me and offer me the admiration that you would like to snatch from me, well, I can do nothing about it; it's not my fault. The field is yours; I'm not responsible for the fact that you are unattractive.

Arsinoé
Oh dear! Do you imagine that I care about this crowd of lovers you are so proud of, or that I don't know how easily they are bought? Do you think you can make us believe that you attract this mob just because you're so alluring? That their love for you is honorable, and that they're courting you because of your virtues? Shoddy merchandise never deceives anyone. We're not dupes. I've seen plenty of women who could inspire true love who still don't have admirers. Everyone knows perfectly well that love must be bought, and at a high price; no one sighs just because of our beautiful eyes. Don't boast about acquiring fake jewels; don't be so proud of your charms. Stop sneering

at people. If I envied your conquests, I could be as wanton as everyone else and show you that anyone who wants can have lovers.

Célimène
Have them by all means, Madame, and we will see how things go; make every effort to please, and without . . .

Arsinoé
Let's stop this conversation, Madame; it is too taxing for both of us. I would have excused myself long ago if my carriage had been ready.

Célimène
Stay as long as you like, Madame; nothing need make you hurry away. I won't bore you by continuing; instead, I'll present to you someone better than I. This gentleman, who by good fortune has just arrived, will entertain you better than I can. Alceste, I must go and write a quick letter that I cannot put off any longer. Please stay with Madame; she will be kind enough to excuse my impoliteness.

Scene 5

ALCESTE, ARSINOÉ

Arsinoé
As you see, she would like me to keep you company for a moment until my coach arrives. Nothing could please me more. You know, people of superior qualities stimulate love and esteem in one another. And your merit, I confess, prompts me to support you in every possible way. I do wish that the Court would pay more attention to your excellence and acknowledge it. You have reason to complain, and I certainly do, when no one makes any efforts on your behalf.

Alceste
I, Madame? And what could I complain about? Has anyone seen me be of service to the State? How I could complain that the Court fails to recognize me; what extraordinary thing have I done?

Arsinoé
Not everyone who is promoted has done something extraordinary. Promotion depends on opportunity as well as on ability. The excellence that you demonstrate should . . .

Alceste
Oh Lord! Let's stop talking about my merit, please. Why should the Court be bothered with that? It would be

overwhelmed if it were obliged to reveal everyone's hidden merit.

Arsinoé
Dazzling merit reveals itself; many people talk about yours. And you should know that in two highly regarded places you were loudly praised by very important people.

Alceste
Eh, Madame! These days everyone is praised and all standards are confused. Everyone is equally meritorious—it's no longer an honor to be honored. People spew out praise, fling it at you; my valet himself was mentioned in the *Gazette*'s society pages.

Arsinoé
For my part, I wish there were some important position at Court that would attract you. If you'd consider it, all you'd have to do is nod and we'd set the wheels in motion. I know the right people; I'd put them to work for you and you'd find the path quite clear.

Alceste
And what would you have me do in this important position? Heaven didn't endow me with a soul that is comfortable at Court. Given my temperament, I'd do better to banish myself. I lack the skills to succeed in these matters. My greatest talent is being direct and sincere; I don't know how to use tricky language to manipulate others. And those who don't know how to hide what they think shouldn't be living in this country. Away from Court one has no friends and titles like the ones you describe; but, having lost these advantages, one also loses the misfortune of dealing with such people, swallowing a thousand dreadful frustrations, praising Monsieur So-and-So's verses, burning incense at the altar of Madame Somebody, and enduring the stupidities of these honorable noblemen.

The Misanthrope, Act III, scene 5

Arsinoé
Well, if you insist, let us stop talking about the Court. Let me say that I grieve when I think of your misplaced love, and, to tell you the truth, I wish that you had been attracted to a far better person. You deserve a happier fate; the woman you love is unworthy of you.

Alceste
When you say that, do you remember that this woman is one of your friends?

Arsinoé
Yes; but my conscience cannot let me continue to see you suffer the wrongs being done to you. Your situation wounds my soul; I must warn you that your beloved is betraying you.

Alceste
How very kind of you, Madame, and how pleasant such information is to a lover!

Arsinoé
Yes, even though she is my friend, I say bluntly that she is unworthy of a gallant man. She only pretends to love you.

Alceste
That may be, Madame; we cannot see into the heart. But it might have been kinder to avoid putting such thoughts in my head.

Arsinoé
If you do not want to know the truth, it's easy enough to say nothing more.

Alceste
No; but in affairs of the heart, doubt is more dreadful than anything else. I would prefer not to be told something unless there's proof that I can see with my own eyes.

The Misanthrope, Act III, scene 5

Arsinoé
Very well, enough said; you'll learn all you need about this matter soon enough. Yes, I want you to trust your eyes. Pray, escort me home, where I'll show you reliable proof of your beloved's disloyalty. And if you were inclined to look elsewhere, one might be able to offer you some consolation.

Act IV

Scene 1

ÉLIANTE, PHILINTE

Philinte
No, I've never seen a more stubborn man, and I've never had so much trouble in reaching a settlement. We tried unsuccessfully to change his mind, but we couldn't shake him. I suspect that the judges have never seen a more bizarre case. "No, Messieurs," he said, "I will not take back what I said, though I'm willing to agree with everything—except for this one point. What offends him? What is he trying to tell me? Is his honor diminished if he doesn't write well? Why does my opinion matter to him; why does he take it the wrong way? One can be a reputable person and still write bad verses; such things have nothing to do with one's honor. I know him to be a fine fellow in all respects: good family, good abilities, a good heart—anything you'd like—but he's a very poor writer. If you like, I'll praise his elegance, his generosity, his horsemanship, his fencing, his dancing; but praise his verses? Please excuse me. And if one isn't fortunate enough to write well, one shouldn't try—unless one's condemned to do so on pain of

death." Well, try as we did to make him soften his tone, all he would say was, "Monsieur, I am sorry to be so difficult, and, since I like you very much, I very much wish I could think your sonnet better than it is." At which point, they embraced one another and we quickly wrapped up the whole business.

Éliante
His behavior is certainly strange, but I admit that there's something remarkable about him. The sincerity that he boasts of — it is, in some ways, noble, even heroic. It's a rare virtue these days; I wish everyone were like him.

Philinte
I must say that the more I see him, the more I'm astonished by the way he has fallen in love. Given his nature, I can't understand how he can love at all, and even less how he came to devote himself to your cousin.

Éliante
It just shows that love doesn't depend on similar temperaments. In his case the usual explanations for falling in love are quite irrelevant.

Philinte
But do you believe, from what you've seen, that he is loved?

Éliante
It's not easy to tell; how could we know whether she truly loves him? Her own heart isn't sure of what it feels; sometimes she's in love without knowing it, and thinks she loves when she doesn't.

Philinte
I think that our friend will be more unhappy with your cousin than he imagines. To tell the truth, if I were he, I would turn my attention elsewhere. He would be wiser, Madame, to respond to the kindness you have shown him.

The Misanthrope, Act IV, scene 1

Éliante
Well, I don't believe in pretense; in such circumstances one should act honestly. I don't make light of his feelings—not at all. I have his best interests at heart and if I could, I'd unite him with the woman he loves. But if the woman he chose were to reject him—which can happen—I would not be unhappy. If he were willing to love someone else, I myself would gladly accept his proposals.

Philinte
And I, Madame, am well aware of your merits, which so attract his attention. If he were willing, he could tell you what I've said to him about you. But if he were to marry your cousin, rather than to devote himself to you, I dare to hope I might be the object of the affection that he rejected. Then I would consider myself truly blessed.

Éliante
You are joking, Philinte.

Philinte
No, Madame, this comes from my heart; believe me—I'm waiting impatiently for the right time to propose to you openly.

Scene 2

ALCESTE, ÉLIANTE, PHILINTE

Alceste
Ah, support me, Madame; I've received a wound that has shattered my heart.

Éliante
What's the matter? What has happened to upset you so much?

Alceste
Something that I cannot believe and still live. No natural catastrophe could destroy me as completely as this has. It is . . . my love . . . I don't know what to say . . .

Éliante
Try to take hold of yourself.

Alceste
My God! Can such grace be linked to such depravity?

Éliante
But what . . . ?

Alceste
Everything is ruined. I am — I am betrayed, stabbed to death. Célimène . . . Can I believe it? Célimène has deceived me, is unfaithful.

The Misanthrope, Act IV, scene 2

Éliante
Have you solid evidence of this?

Philinte
Perhaps this is just some foolish suspicion; your jealousy sometimes invents monsters . . .

Alceste
Damn it, Monsieur! Mind your own business. The proof of her treachery is all too clear—look, here in my pocket, in her own handwriting, a letter she wrote to Oronte: that's the evidence of my disgrace and her shame. Yes, Oronte, whom I thought she was trying to avoid, the one I thought was the last person I needed to fear.

Philinte
A letter may appear to be something it's not; it's often less serious than it seems.

Alceste
Monsieur, please, once again, leave me alone; don't meddle with things that do not concern you.

Éliante
Try to be calm; this rage . . .

Alceste
Calming me is your task, Madame. I turn to you now—help end my suffering. Take vengeance upon your cowardly, ungrateful, treacherous cousin who has toyed with my affections; avenge me for this act that must surely horrify you.

Éliante
Avenge? I? How?

The Misanthrope, Act IV, scene 2

Alceste
By accepting my love. Accept it, Madame, replace that faithless woman. This is how I will be avenged; I will punish her by my sincere devotion, by the deep love, by the respectful attention, by my eagerness to serve, by sacrificing my heart to you.

Éliante
I certainly sympathize with your suffering; I value the heart that you offer. Still, possibly the harm isn't as great as you imagine; you might be able to abandon your demand for vengeance. When people we love seem to injure us we may want to retaliate—but that feeling will pass. Perhaps we think we have good reason to reject them, but they soon enough seem innocent to us. The wound will heal; everyone knows about lovers' heartaches.

Alceste
No, no, Madame, this is a deadly blow, there's no turning back. I've broken with her forever. Nothing can change my plan; I would hate myself if I continued to love her.—Here she is; the closer she comes the worse I feel. I'll accuse her of her crimes, confront her openly, and then I will offer you a heart free of her deceitful charms.

Scene 3

CÉLIMÈNE, ALCESTE

Alceste
O Heavens! Can I master my rage?

Célimène
Oof! Why do you seem so upset? What's the meaning of these sighs and those somber glances?

Alceste
No evil of which the human soul is capable can be compared to your disloyalty. No fate, no demon, no angry Heaven has ever created a being as wicked as you.

Célimène
Your kindness is admirable.

Alceste
No witticisms, please; this is no laughing matter. You would do better to blush: I have certain proof of your treachery. This explains my misery; not for nothing was I anxious. My suspicions, which some found offensive, prompted me to look for harm, and I found it. Despite your caution, your ability to pretend, my instincts told me what I ought to fear. Don't assume that I will put up with this outrageous betrayal without taking revenge. Yes, I know: desire can't be controlled; love

can come unbidden; a heart can't be captured by force; it's free to choose its master. If you had told me the truth, if you had sent me away at the start, I would have had no cause for complaint. But encouraging me deceitfully—that is treachery, that is a crime for which no punishment is enough. I have a right to be resentful. I'm warning you; this blow is killing me. I can't stop myself; reason doesn't control my emotions now. Yes: I am overwhelmed by anger; I am justifiably enraged; I will not be responsible for what I might do.

Célimène
And what accounts for this frenzy? Have you lost your wits?

Alceste
Yes indeed I have. Just the sight of you infected me with deadly poison, the poison of believing that your fraudulent, bewitching behavior was sincere.

Célimène
What is this treachery that you complain about?

Alceste
Ah, the heart is above all things deceitful . . . Well, I have evidence to put an end to all this. Look—do you recognize your handwriting? This letter that I found is enough to condemn you; there's no defense against this evidence.

Célimène
Is this what's bothering you?

Alceste
You don't blush when you see what you have written?

Célimène
Why should I blush?

The Misanthrope, Act IV, scene 3

Alceste
What? Are you brazen as well as deceitful? Do you deny it's yours, just because it isn't signed?

Célimène
Why should I deny writing a letter?

Alceste
What? It reveals your crime and you can look at it without being embarrassed?

Célimène
I must say, you really are behaving like a madman.

Alceste
What? You challenge this unimpeachable evidence? The way it demonstrates your affection for Oronte—shouldn't that enrage me and shame you?

Célimène
Oronte! Who told you that it was addressed to him?

Alceste
The people who gave it to me today. And even if it is addressed to someone else, have I no right to complain? Would you be less guilty?

Célimène
And if I wrote it to a woman: how could that harm you? Of what am I guilty?

Alceste
Oh, that's a clever way to escape—something that I didn't expect, I must admit. And so here I am, completely convinced. How dare you use such a shabby trick? Do you think people are so blind? Come, come, let's watch you twist and turn and

pretend so that you can improve upon such an obvious lie —
your claim that you wrote this passionate letter to a woman.
If you want to clear yourself of disloyalty, then explain, if you
please, what I'm about to read . . .

Célimène
It does not please me. I find you quite ridiculous when you
bully me and say such things to my face.

Alceste
Now, now: without losing your temper, just explain the words
written here.

Célimène
No, I don't want to, and in any event I don't really care what
you think.

Alceste
I beg you, explain to me how a letter like this could be written
to a woman and I'll be satisfied.

Célimène
No, it's written to Oronte, and I want everyone to believe it.
I enjoy his attention, I admire what he says, I value him, and
I agree with anything you'd like. Please, go off, don't let me
delay you. And please stop screaming at me.

Alceste
Dear Heaven! Has anything more cruel ever been created?
Has any heart ever been treated this way? What? I'm
justifiably angry with her, I come to plead my case, and I'm the
one who is attacked! I'm devoured by grief and suspicion; I'm
allowed to believe things while others smile about it: and I'm a
coward, I'm chained to her and can't break away, I can't bring
myself to denounce someone whom I still love. Oh, you know
all too well how to use my weakness against me, how to take

The Misanthrope, Act IV, scene 3

advantage of my desperate love for you. Acquit yourself of a crime that devastates me, stop pretending to be guilty—let me believe in the innocence of that letter. I love you, I'll meet you halfway; do your best to seem faithful, and I, for my part, will do my best to believe you.

Célimène
Come, come: this jealous rage has made you mad; you scarcely deserve to be loved. What could possibly make me degrade myself by deceiving you? If I began to love someone else, why wouldn't I tell you the truth? Can't my willingness to reassure you overcome your doubts? Does my assurance mean nothing? Aren't you insulting me by believing your suspicions? A woman's honor prevents her from admitting desire; it's only after a struggle that we are able to confess that we love. And if a lover hears such a confession, how dare he distrust it? Isn't he wrong to doubt what she says? When I listen to your suspicions I feel I'm right to be angry; you don't deserve to be taken seriously. I'm annoyed at myself for being foolish and weak enough to continue to care for you. I should look for someone else and give you a legitimate reason to complain.

Alceste
Oh, you traitor! Loving you is pure insanity. There's no doubt you're deceiving me with these sweet phrases, but what can I do? I must submit to my fate. I surrender to you; I'm determined to believe you. Come what may I'll see how it all ends, I'll see what your heart is like, and whether it will be corrupt enough to betray me.

Célimène
No. You do not love me as one ought to love.

Alceste
Ah . . . no one has ever loved as intensely as I. My love is so strong that it has even made me wish you ill. Yes, I wish that

The Misanthrope, Act IV, scene 3

no one liked you, that you were reduced to a miserable life, that Heaven had robbed you of everything—rank, family, wealth—so that I could have the joy of knowing that my glorious sacrifices had repaired your misfortunes, and that everything you had was due to me.

Célimène
That's a strange way to wish me well! Heaven forbid that you should succeed . . . But here is Monsieur Du Bois, looking rather odd.

Scene 4

Du Bois, Célimène, Alceste

Alceste
What's all this fuss? Why do you look so frightened? What's the matter with you?

Du Bois
Monsieur . . .

Alceste
Well?

Du Bois
This is a very mysterious business.

Alceste
What's all this?

Du Bois
Monsieur, we're in trouble up to our ears.

Alceste
What?

Du Bois
Can I speak out loud?

The Misanthrope, Act IV, scene 4

Alceste
Yes, talk, and talk quickly.

Du Bois
Isn't there someone who . . .

Alceste
Ugh! What nonsense! Will you please speak up?

Du Bois
Monsieur, we have to beat a retreat.

Alceste
What?

Du Bois
No drums or trumpets, just retreat.

Alceste
And why?

Du Bois
I tell you we have to leave this place.

Alceste
The reason?

Du Bois
We have to go—no time for good-byes.

Alceste
But why are you telling me this?

Du Bois
Because we have to start to pack.

The Misanthrope, Act IV, scene 4

Alceste
I'll crack your head open if you don't start to explain yourself, you scoundrel.

Du Bois
Monsieur, a man with a scowl as black as his clothes came — right into our kitchen — to leave us a piece of paper scrawled so badly that only a demon could decipher it. I'm quite sure it has to do with your lawsuit — but the devil himself probably couldn't understand it all.

Alceste
Well . . . what . . . what's in this paper, and what does it have to do with this departure you're talking about?

Du Bois
What I'm talking about is that an hour ago a man who often comes to visit came to find you in a great hurry, and, since he didn't find you, he politely instructed me — knowing that I serve you with much zeal — to tell you that: wait, what was his name?

Alceste
Never mind about his name, you fool; tell me what he said.

Du Bois
Well, at any rate, it was one of your friends. He said that the danger you're in means you have to run, and that you're threatened with being arrested.

Alceste
But wait — wasn't he more specific?

Du Bois
No. He asked for paper and some ink and wrote a few words that will explain this mystery to you.

Alceste
Well, give it to me.

Célimène
What is all this about?

Alceste
I don't know, but I hope to be enlightened; will you hurry up, you wretch?

Du Bois [*Having searched his pockets for a long time.*]
My word! I think, Monsieur, I left it on your table.

Alceste
I don't know why I don't . . .

Célimène
Don't lose your temper; hurry to disentangle yourself from this mess.

Alceste
It seems that no matter what I do, fate has decided that I cannot have a conversation with you. Well, I'll prevail, and, for the sake of my love, permit me, Madame, to return before the end of the day.

Act V

Scene 1

ALCESTE, PHILINTE

Alceste
I've made my mind up, I tell you.

Philinte
But whatever it was, do you have to . . .

Alceste:
You can do and say anything you like—nothing can stop me. We live in a corrupt age, and I will not have anything more to do with humanity. Look—honor, virtue, decency, and the laws all support my case; everyone says that my cause is just; I feel secure in my rights—and I have failed. Justice is on my side, and I lost the case! A wretch whose scandalous history is well known has won because of a damned lie! Integrity gave in to treachery! He has destroyed me and found a way to exonerate himself. Those smirks and pretenses, so brilliantly contrived, have simply turned justice inside out. And he's topped off his crime by procuring a summons against me! And as if robbing

The Misanthrope, Act V, scene 1

me of my rights weren't enough, he's circulating a scandalous book—even reading it is a crime—a book that should be censored ruthlessly—and he claims that I wrote it! And as a result, here's Oronte who's whispering and trying to peddle this forgery! Oronte, who has the reputation of being an honorable man, to whom I did nothing other than to be sincere and frank—Oronte, who came to me uninvited and pushed me to tell him what I thought of his verses—Oronte, who's helping to accuse me of some invented crime because I was honest and refused to deceive him or to lie—Oronte has become my worst enemy! He'll never forgive me because I didn't say that his sonnet was good! And all men—damn it—are like that! They do things like that for the sake of fame! This is what they mean by good faith, by virtue, zeal, justice, and honor! Right: I've put up long enough with these horrors. I'm leaving this jungle of cutthroats. Since you live like wolves, you traitors, you'll no longer have me living with you.

Philinte
I think you are being a bit hasty. Things aren't as bad as all that. You haven't been arrested, despite the accusation your opponent had the audacity to make. You'll see: his lies will destroy him; he could well be ruined by what he did.

Alceste
He? He's not afraid of playing these tricks; he's been given permission to be a villain. Harmed by what he did? Far from it! You'll see that tomorrow he'll be in an even better position.

Philinte
Look, it's obvious that no one takes seriously his malicious rumors about you. In that respect you have nothing to fear. And as for your case, about which you can well complain, you can easily appeal, and as for this warrant . . .

The Misanthrope, Act V, scene 1

Alceste
No, I will certainly not change my mind, I will certainly not challenge the warrant. We see justice betrayed too often; well, I want this to be a warning to posterity, clear evidence of how corrupt men are today. It will cost me twenty thousand francs; well, for twenty thousand francs I will have the right to curse the inhuman human race and to keep my hatred alive.

Philinte
But really . . .

Alceste
But really . . . your efforts are useless. What, Monsieur, is there to be said about all this? Are you brazen enough to want to make excuses for all the loathsome things that have happened?

Philinte
No, I'll agree with anything you want. Things only succeed because of intrigue and self-interest; success depends on chicanery; men should have been created differently. But is their injustice a good reason to withdraw from society? Human failures give us ways to test our philosophy of life; that's what virtue is for. If everyone were honorable, open, just, well-behaved, most of our virtues would be useless. We only need them to help us tolerate the faults of others. And just as a purely virtuous heart . . .

Alceste
You present these things, dear Monsieur, as well as anyone possibly could, and you always have reasonable things to say. But you are wasting your time and your fine speeches. Reason tells me to withdraw for my own good. I can't always control myself, I can't be responsible for what I might say—I could burst out violently and simply make matters worse. Don't argue with me; leave me here to wait for Célimène; it's essential

The Misanthrope, Act V, scene 1

for her to agree to my plans. I'll see if she indeed does love me; this is the moment to test her.

Philinte
Let's go upstairs to Éliante to wait for her.

Alceste
No, I'm too upset. You go to see her; this dark corner is the right place for me and my misery.

Philinte
It's an uncomfortable place to wait; I'll ask Éliante to come down.

Scene 2

Oronte, Célimène, Alceste

Oronte
Yes, dear lady, you must decide whether you are willing to have me devote myself to you. I insist on reliable assurance; a lover does not love uncertainty. If my passion has been able to move you, you must stop pretending and trying to hide the fact. Prove your devotion by forbidding Alceste to court you, give him up for the sake of my love, and banish him from this day on.

Célimène
But why are you so irritated by him—you, whom I've heard praising him so much?

Oronte
Madame, I am not obliged to explain myself to you. The issue is to know your feelings. Choose, please, one or the other of us: my decision depends only on yours.

Alceste [*Coming out of the corner into which he had withdrawn.*]
Yes, this gentleman is right: Madame, you must choose; his demands match my own. The same passion, the same anxiety brings me here; my love wants assurance of your own. Matters can no longer drag on this way: this is the time to declare yourself.

Oronte
I do not want my tiresome emotions to impair your own good fortune, Monsieur.

Alceste
I am not jealous, Monsieur; I simply do not want to share any part of her heart with you.

Oronte [*To Alceste.*]
If she prefers your love to mine . . .

Alceste
If she gives you the slightest sign . . .

Oronte
I swear I'll make no further claim.

Alceste
I swear I won't see her again.

Oronte
Madame, speak out, no hesitation.

Alceste
Madame, no more equivocation.

Oronte
You've only to say which you prefer.

Alceste
Make your choice; we'll concur.

Oronte
What? Do you insist we wait?

Alceste
What? Do you still debate?

The Misanthrope, Act V, scene 2

Célimène
Good heavens! What rude, ridiculous behavior! You both seem demented! I have no doubt about whom I prefer; my heart isn't swinging back and forth between the two of you. It was quite easy to make a decision. But I feel very uncomfortable declaring myself publicly, and I don't think that unpleasant remarks should be made in front of others. A heart can make its choice known without insulting someone. I prefer to dismiss a lover more gently.

Oronte
No, no, I have no fear of a frank confession; I'm willing to hear it.

Alceste
And I insist on it. Blurt it out; I don't want you to be tactful. You take pleasure in protecting everyone; well, no more games, no more ambiguity. You must explain yourself. If you are silent, I'll take that as a decision and assume that the worst I could imagine has in fact been said.

Oronte
I'm grateful, Monsieur, that you have been so outspoken, and I would have said the same things as you have.

Célimène
How you tire me with your foolishness. Is it fair to be so demanding? Haven't I explained why I hold back? Here is Éliante; let her be the judge.

Scene 3

ÉLIANTE, PHILINTE, CÉLIMÈNE,
ORONTE, ALCESTE

Célimène
Dear cousin, I find myself besieged by people who seem to share the same bad mood. Each insists that I disclose which one I prefer, and announce, in their presence, which one I forbid to continue wooing me. Tell me, have you ever heard of such a thing?

Éliante
Don't ask me to decide such things. You've chosen the wrong person: I vote for those who speak their minds.

Oronte [*To Célimène.*]
Madame, your defenses are in vain.

Alceste
Madame, evasion causes pain.

Oronte
Madame, stop wavering and choose.

Alceste
Madame, you may refuse.

The Misanthrope, Act V, scene 3

Oronte
I need to hear your voice, Madame.

Alceste
I think I know your choice.

Last Scene

ACASTE, CLITANDRE, ARSINOÉ,
PHILINTE, ÉLIANTE, ORONTE,
CÉLIMÈNE, ALCESTE

Acaste
Madame, we've both come — I hope this is not an intrusion — to clear up a little matter.

Clitandre
What good luck, Messieurs, to find you here, since you too are involved in this matter.

Arsinoé
Madame, you may be surprised to see me, but these gentlemen insisted upon it. Both came to me, both complained about something that I can scarcely believe. I respect you too much to think that you could commit a crime like this one. My eyes refuse to believe the evidence, though it does seem persuasive. Since I believe that little disagreements should not destroy friendship, I was quite happy to come and watch you clear yourself of slander.

Acaste
Yes, Madame, can you calmly justify this? Did you write this letter to Clitandre?

The Misanthrope, Act V, last scene

Clitandre
Did you write this charming letter to Acaste?

Acaste
You'll recognize this handwriting, Messieurs, and, given its style, I don't believe you'll have trouble knowing who wrote it. It is worth reading:

> *You are a strange fellow to complain about my high spirits, and to accuse me of being happy only when I'm not with you. Nothing could be further from the truth; and if you do not come promptly to beg pardon for offending me, I will not forgive you as long as I live. That great booby the Viscount...*

He should be here.

> *That great booby the Viscount, of whom you complained at the start, is a man I hope never to see again. Since the time I watched him spend three quarters of an hour spitting into a well just to watch the ripples, I have never been able to think well of him. As for the little Marquis...*

Without being boastful, I'd say it's my turn...

> *As for the little Marquis who held my hand for such a long time yesterday—what a lightweight. His merits? Not worth a penny. As for the man with the green ribbons...*[12]

It's your turn, sir.

> *As for the man with the green ribbons, he amuses me from time to time with his abruptness and his peevish complaints; but there are hundreds of times when I think he's the most annoying man alive. And the man with the vest...*[13]

---

12. This is usually taken to be a reference to Alceste.
13. Notes indicate that this referred to the costume that Oronte wore in the first performances; in subsequent editions Molière called him "the man who wrote that sonnet."

The Misanthrope, Act V, last scene

This bit's for you.

> *The man with the vest, who thinks he's a wit, and wants to be an author no matter what: I can't be bothered to listen to him; and his prose bores me as much as his verses do. Please understand: I'm not having quite as much fun as you think. I find myself saying more than I want when I'm dragged to parties; and I believe the only way to enjoy oneself is to be with people whom one likes.*

Clitandre
And now it's my turn.

> *Your Clitandre, of whom you speak, and who wants to be my sweetheart, is the last man whose friendship I want. His fantasy is that he is loved, and yours is to imagine that you are not. Exchange fantasies with him, and see me as often as you can to help me bear the discomfort of his being obsessed with me.*[14]

Here's the work of an exemplary human being, and do you know her name, Madame? Enough: we'll be off to show everyone this flattering portrait of your character.

Acaste
I'd be justified in saying something about this, Madame, but I don't think you're worth being angry about. I'll show you: a "little marquis" can console himself with others more deserving of his love.

Oronte
What? Is this how I'm insulted, after all the things you wrote to me? And now you offer your phony love to anyone who comes along? Right: I was duped, but I won't be any more.

---

14. With some variation, this scene is repeated in Wycherley's *The Plain Dealer*, Act IV, scene 2.

The Misanthrope, Act V, last scene

You've done me a world of good by letting me know what you are. Fortunately, I'm not heartbroken, and your loss is my gain. [*To Alceste.*] Monsieur, I won't stand in your way; you can continue your affair with Madame.

Arsinoé
This is the vilest deed in all of history; I'm deeply upset; I won't be able to stop talking about it. Has anyone seen such behavior? I don't meddle in others' affairs, but Monsieur, here, who assured your happiness, a man like this, full of merit and honor, honorable, who idolized you, must he . . .

Alceste
Please allow me, Madame, to take care of my own interests; you need not come to my defense. I'm in no position to reward you; and if I wanted to take revenge by choosing someone else to love, it surely would not be you.

Arsinoé
Ho! Do you imagine, Monsieur, that one might have dreamed of such a thing, or be so eager to accept you? If you really believe what you said, then you're the most arrogant person alive. Who would want something that this lady has discarded? Don't deceive yourself; get off your high horse. You don't deserve someone like me. Go on, sigh for her, do; I'm eager to watch the results of this fine match. [*She leaves.*]

Alceste
Well, I have been silent despite what I have seen; I let everyone else speak first. Have I controlled myself long enough, may I now . . . ?

Célimène
Yes, you may say what you like. You have the right to complain, to find fault with me. I am in the wrong; I confess it. I am ashamed of myself; I won't try to buy you off with

The Misanthrope, Act V, last scene

empty excuses. I'm not disturbed when others attack me, but I agree that I have acted shamefully toward you. You may well be displeased; I know how guilty I appear, that everything suggests that I was capable of betraying you; you are entitled to hate me. Do: I consent.

Alceste
Oh! You traitor, could I do such a thing? Do you think I can stifle my emotions? And even if I wanted with all my heart to hate you, is my heart ready to obey me? [*To Éliante and Philinte.*] You see what shameful love can do to a man; you're witnesses to my weakness. But you haven't seen everything; I'm about to go farther, to show you how foolish it is to claim to be wise. In the end, all we are is human. Yes, you sorcerer, I can make excuses for your crime: I will convince myself it was only the weakness of a young woman influenced by the vices of the times. I'll forgive you if you are willing to adopt my plan, to abandon society, to live with me hidden deep in the country. That is the only place where you can repair the damage your letter has caused; after this disgraceful episode, it's only there that I could love you again.

Célimène
I! Renounce the world before I'm an old woman? Bury myself in your splendid isolation?

Alceste
And if your emotions are like mine, why do you need the rest of the world? Am I not enough to satisfy you?

Célimène
Solitude is frightening to a twenty-year-old; I don't feel strong enough to be able to take such a step. If giving you my hand is enough to satisfy you, I could do that, and marriage . . .

The Misanthrope, Act V, last scene

Alceste
No. Now I detest you. You refuse: that has affected me more than anything else you could have done. Since I by myself cannot satisfy you, as you by yourself would satisfy me, I reject you. This insult frees me from the shameful love I had for someone so unworthy. [*Célimène leaves, and Alceste speaks to Éliante.*] Madame, your virtues, your sincerity, enhance your beauty. I have admired you; let me continue to respect you. But in these difficult moments, I must withdraw. I know I am unworthy of you, and I begin to understand that Heaven did not create me for marriage. It would be wrong to offer a heart that does not deserve you, and indeed . . .

Éliante
You need say no more. If I were to offer my hand it would be to your friend here, who would, I believe, accept it without hesitation.

Philinte
Oh, Madame, I have always hoped for such an honor, and I would sacrifice everything to gain it.

Alceste
May you both continue to feel this way, and enjoy true happiness! But I, betrayed at every turn, overwhelmed by injustice, I will leave this hellhole where vice is triumphant, and find some lonely spot where I may live freely as an honorable man. [*Alceste leaves.*]

Philinte
Come, Madame, let us do our best to stop this plan of his.

The End

Notes to *The Misanthrope*

Note on the Names of Characters in *The Misanthrope*

As in *Tartuffe,* the names in *The Misanthrope* seem largely to echo the traditions of the *Précieuses,* the learned ladies of Molière's day whose elaborate novels, set in an imagined ancient world, presented heroes and heroines whose names seemed derived from Greek and Latin classics. Some of Molière's names suggest a meaning: "Alceste" comes from a Greek root meaning "valiant" or "strong," "Philinte" can be translated as "lover of humanity," "Arsinoé" is the name for a succession of Greek wives of Egyptian rulers (many of whom had disastrous or corrupt marriages). As in *Tartuffe,* Molière seems to be using such names to propose that his characters reflect universal traits.

Names in the English Restoration comedies, which were written at almost the same time as Molière's comedies and often drew heavily on his plays, are less far-fetched but follow the same pattern. William Wycherley's *The Plain Dealer,* parts of which are almost literal translations of *The Misanthrope,* includes figures called Manly, My Lord Plausible, Major Oldfox, and Fidelia. Wycherley's contemporaries used the same device: Colley Cibber's *Love's Last Shift* presents Sir William Wisewoud, Loveless, and two servants, Snap and Sly. Some of the best occur in Sir John Vanbrugh's *The Relapse:* Sir Novelty Fashion, Newly Created Lord Foppinton; Worthy, a Gentleman of the Town; Sir Tunbelly Clumsey, a Country Gentleman; Miss Hoyden, a Great Fortune, Daughter to Sir Tunbelly. This tradition of names appeared in England as early as the medieval "mystery" plays, whose characters were Everyman, Fellowship, Knowledge, and Beauty. John Bunyan, writing at almost the same time as Molière, called his hero Christian and had him encounter Mr. Worldly Wiseman, the Giant Despair, and Faithful.

These figures are entangled in schemes, reversals, sudden recognitions; the names help the spectators follow the complicated plots and even anticipate the endings. The advantages of this shorthand are obvious. At the same time, using such names can force a kind of straitjacket on the characters. Brilliant as is much of the dialogue in the Restoration comedies, the characters themselves do not evolve; nor do Alceste, Philinte, or Éliante. Holding up a mirror to society, is Molière suggesting that the characteristics of the actors—on and off the stage—are more fixed, less free to develop and change than he, or they, might wish?

Act I, scene 2: Oronte's Sonnet: a line-by-line more literal translation

L'espoir, il est vrai, nous soulage, Hope, it is true, comforts us,
Et nous berce un temps notre ennui; And lulls our worries a while;
Mais, Philis, le triste avantage, But Philis, that help is no use,
Lorsque rien ne marche après lui! If nothing comes of it all.

Vous eûtes de la complaisance; You once had some kindness,
Mais vous en deviez moins avoir, But you should have had less of it.
Et ne vous pas mettre en dépense And you shouldn't have taken such pains
Pour ne me donner que l'espoir. Since you offer me nothing but hope.

S'il faut qu'une attente éternelle If all this endless waiting
Pousse à bout l'ardeur de mon zèle, Pushes my love to its end
Le trépas sera mon recours. Death is the only recourse.

The Misanthrope, Notes: Act 1, scene 2

Vos soins ne m'en peuvent distraire: Your efforts cannot change my mind:

Belle Philis, on désespère   Dear Philis, one loses all hope
Alors qu'on espère toujours.   If one hopes endlessly.

Act I, scene 2: *If King Henry . . .*

*If King Henry were to say, "Paris shall be yours today,
But you'll have to go away from your true beloved,"*

Si le roi m'avait donné "Paris sa grand' ville,
Et qu'il me fallût quitter l'amour de ma mie,"

*I would tell King Henry then "Take your Paris back again.
I prefer my one true love! I love my beloved."*

Je dirais au roi Henri, "Reprenez votre Paris,
J'aime mieux ma mie, au gué! J'aime mieux ma mie."

Act II, scene 1: of Lawsuits in *The Misanthrope*

Two, perhaps three lawsuits in one play? This pattern, together with the appearance of notaries and officers of the court in Molière's other comedies, invites attention. Grimarest, Molière's first biographer, reports that many people believed that Molière had studied the law, basing their assertions on remarks made by Molière's widow or daughter. Others, who claimed to know Molière well, argue that he had had no such training.[1] A recently discovered collection of court documents indicates that in 1645 Molière was twice imprisoned briefly, the first time for nonpayment of a debt, the second on a trumped-up charge of assault.[2] Yet although the playwright may have been reflecting his own tangles with the law in *The Misanthrope*, Alceste's and Célimène's responses to their legal difficulties seem to bear on larger issues.

In other plays by Molière the notaries and court officials come on the stage with their robes and staves of office. Their language is pompous or abrupt; some appear obsequious, others unsure of themselves. Like Molière's physicians, they are caricatures rather than fully realized characters, appropriate subjects for comedy. In *The Misanthrope*, however, they are referred to but not seen. In Act I Philinte asks Alceste whether he will call on the judges before whom his case will appear. No, says Alceste: is my case unjust or in doubt? Philinte warns Alceste that a cabal could produce a verdict condemning him—a warning that Molière knew to be grounded in reality. A cabal that marshaled against him the forces of religious orthodoxy and some of the King's counselors had, after all, banned *Tartuffe* from the stage for five years.

Philinte asks Alceste who will argue his case for him; Alceste replies, "Reason, my rights, equity . . . I'll see, during the trial, whether those men have enough gall, are wicked, conniving,

---

1. See Grimarest, *La Vie de M. De Molière*, Édition critique par Georges Mongrédien (Paris: Michel Brient, 1955), 128.
2. See *Revue d'histoire du théâtre* IV (1972): 351–54.

and corrupt enough to perpetrate an injustice that all the world would recognize. . . . Even if it costs me a fortune, I'm willing to lose the case just for the satisfaction of it." Alceste's defiance, like Célimène's excuse for encouraging Clitandre in Act II—"he promises to use his friends to help me in the lawsuit I'm involved in"—reveals the differences between Molière's characters. It also allows Molière to take aim at an aspect of society that enrages Alceste and, perhaps, some members of his audience.

Act II, scene 4: Éliante's Speech

"Lovers always boast about those they love," says Éliante. Behind her gentle mockery is a direct reference both to the society of her days and to the world of the first century BCE. Éliante (or her model) may not have been a friend of Mlle. de Scudéry, one of the most elegant leaders of Parisian society. Mlle. de Scudéry, however, knew and appreciated Molière's work; in her fictional "conversation" about hypocrisy, one of the speakers explicitly mentions Molière's *Tartuffe*.[3] Éliante's speech and the exchanges in the earlier part of Act II, scene 4, have the flavor of Mlle. de Scudéry's lengthy novels and reported conversations, which were constructed in the elaborate language of the *Précieuses*, those highly educated women whose salons influenced the court and the nobility. Molière's comic exaggeration of their ambitions first appeared in his early play *Les Précieuses Ridicules* (*The Ridiculous Affected Ladies*), and he returned to the topic in a much later play, *Les Femmes Savantes* (*The Learned Ladies*). His audiences, female and male, came, laughed at the plays—perhaps a bit uncomfortably—and kept on coming; the receipts testify to their interest in women's intellectual ambition and its distortions.

---

3. *Choix de Conversations de Mlle de Scudéry,* Edité avec une introduction et des notes par Phillip J. Wolfe (Ravenna: Longo Editore, 1977), 147.

As for the first century BCE, Éliante's amusing speech is evidence that she herself is something of a "learned lady." She is echoing very faithfully a passage in *De Rerum Natura*, the long poem by Lucretius that describes what was known and imagined about the natural world—a work well known to students who had had a classical education. Its first three books are directly concerned with the natural world and include an early version of the atomic theory of matter. The fourth book turns to the animal world and to the nature of human beings, their emotions as well as their physiology. In lines 1160–75 Lucretius offers a lover's vocabulary that is remarkably similar to Éliante's. An early biography of Molière mentions an unverified report that Molière prepared a translation of Lucretius, perhaps prompted by his studies with the philosopher Gassendi at the Jesuit Collège de Clermont.[4] It would be interesting to know whether this was true, for it hints at a somewhat surprising element in Molière's formal education: the lines by Lucretius that precede his (and Éliante's) recreation of the beloved are remarkably explicit descriptions of sexual relations.

Ambiguity in *The Misanthrope* (note to the last line of the play)

Ambiguities abound in *The Misanthrope*. Is Philinte a true friend of Alceste, or is he too compliant with the customs of the times, too polite, too evasive? Is Célimène quite as scornful as she seems? Is Éliante—Philinte calls her "true-hearted"—playing games when she describes the ways a lover dismisses the faults in his beloved?

And Alceste: at the end of Act IV, he says to Célimène, "Acquit yourself of a crime that devastates me, stop pretending to be

---

4. Grimarest, *La vie de M. de Molière*, 127–28.

guilty—let me believe in the innocence of that letter. I love you, I'll meet you halfway; do your best to seem faithful, and I, for my part, will do my best to believe you." High standards undermined by love? At the end of Act V he calls her "unworthy" of his love. Was she unworthy? Or are his feelings hurt by her reluctance to follow him into his splendid isolation?

Of all the ambiguities in the play, perhaps the most perplexing presents itself in the last line, spoken by Philinte to Éliante: "Come, Madame, let us do our best to stop this plan of his." Why is Philinte so anxious to stop Alceste? Is disappearing into the countryside a dangerous act? Does Philinte fear that Alceste will do more than go off to his retreat in the provinces—that he might commit suicide?

This last seems barely possible; nothing we have seen of Alceste suggests that he is a physically violent man or one who would take such a desperate final step. But given the importance of city and society in seventeenth-century France, one can imagine that Philinte might think that Alceste's retreat is a kind of emotional self-destruction. France in this period was becoming increasingly centralized, partly in reaction to the conflicts between certain groups of nobles and the king. Once Louis XIV had established his power, Paris was more than ever the heart of political, social, and cultural life in France. In 1658 Molière, who had spent several years with a company of actors touring throughout France, returned to Paris where he had been born, and he never left. Many of his plays (*Tartuffe* is one) include jibes at those who live in the provinces, or those who fail to learn how to behave once they reach the metropolis. A century later, ladies might pretend to be simple shepherdesses for a few days, but for Molière, as for his audiences, life was rooted in and defined by the city. Leaving it voluntarily might at best have seemed ridiculous and at worse insane (a word that originally meant unhealthy). Molière did not write a preface for *The Misanthrope* as he did for *Tartuffe*. It is up to his audiences to interpret for themselves Philinte's last, urgent speech.

Roger W. Herzel is Professor Emeritus in the Department of Theater and Drama at Indiana University, Bloomington. His research specialization is Molière. He is the author of *The Original Casting of Molière's Plays* and of articles in a number of journals including *PMLA*, *Modern Language Notes*, *Seventeenth Century French Studies*, and *Theatre Survey*. He contributed the entries on Molière and sixteen other seventeenth-century French actors to the *Oxford Encyclopedia of Theatre and Performance*. His article on the original cast of Molière's *The Misanthrope* was awarded the William Riley Parker Prize of the Modern Language Association (1980). Professor Herzel was Editor of *Theatre Survey*, the journal of the American Society for Theatre Research, from 1980 to 1990, and Director of Graduate Studies at Indiana University from 1986 to 1997.

Prudence L. Steiner took her Ph.D. at Harvard University, where she served as Lecturer and Director of the Harvard Extension School Writing Program. Between 1953 and 1954 Dr. Steiner studied at the Sorbonne in a program for the training teachers of French as a foreign language. Because the instructors believed that teaching French required a full knowledge of French history and culture, she attended plays—Molière, Racine, Corneille, Marivaux, Victor Hugo, Jean Anouilh, Paul Claudel, and others—at the Comèdie Française, the Théâtre National Populaire, and other theaters in Paris. From this Dr. Steiner developed a continuing interest in and enthusiasm for the classical French theater of which Molière is one of the first and most important creators. Also available from Hackett is her translation of *Voltaire's Philosophical Letters* (2007).